NATURAL DISASTERS

Where I Live

HURRICANES

Tracy Vonder Brink

Teaching Tips for Caregivers and Teachers:

This Hi-Lo book features high-interest subject matter that will appeal to all readers in intermediate and middle school grades. It may be enjoyed by students reading at or above grade level as well as by those who are looking for age-appropriate themes matched with a less challenging reading level. Hi-Lo books are ideal for ELL readers, too.

Each book appeals to a striving reader's age and maturity level. Opportunities are provided for students to read words they already know while encountering a limited number of new, high-interest vocabulary words. With these supports in place, students will read more fluently while increasing reading comprehension. Use the following suggestions to help students grow as readers.

- Encourage the student to read independently at home.
- Encourage the student to practice reading aloud.
- Encourage activities that require reading.
- Establish a regular reading time.
- Have the student write questions about what they read.

Teaching Tips for Teachers:

Before Reading

- Ask, "What do I know about this topic?"
- Ask, "What do I want to learn about this topic?"

During Reading

- Ask, "What is the author trying to teach me?"
- Ask, "How is this like something I already know?"

After Reading

- Discuss how the text features (headings, index, etc.) help with understanding the topic.
- Ask, "What interesting or fun fact did you learn?"

TABLE OF CONTENTS

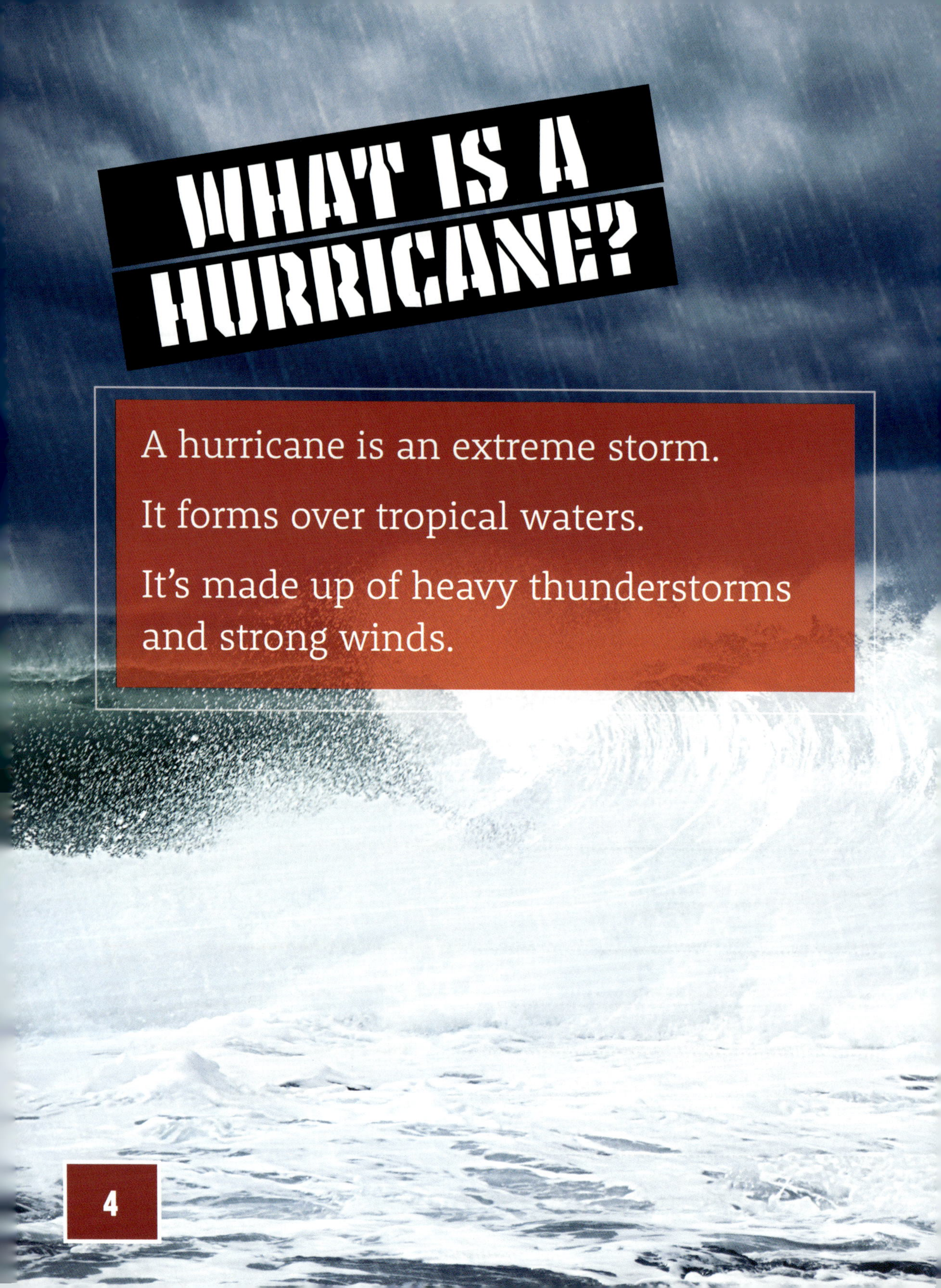

WHAT IS A HURRICANE?

A hurricane is an extreme storm.

It forms over tropical waters.

It's made up of heavy thunderstorms and strong winds.

ATLANTIC OCEAN HURRICANE NAMES				
2022	**2023**	**2024**	**2025**	**2026**
ALEX	ARLENE	ALBERTO	ANDREA	ARTHUR
BONNIE	BRET	BERYL	BARRY	BERTHA
COLIN	CINDY	CHRIS	CHANTAL	CRISTOBAL
DANIELLE	DON	DEBBY	DEXTER	DOLLY
EARL	EMILY	ERNESTO	ERIN	EDOUARD
FIONA	FRANKLIN	FRANCINE	FERNAND	FAY
GASTON	GERT	GORDON	GABRIELLE	GONZALO
HERMINE	HAROLD	HELENE	HUMBERTO	HANNA
IAN	IDALIA	ISAAC	IMELDA	ISAIAS
JULIA	JOSE	JOYCE	JERRY	JOSEPHINE
KARL	KATIA	KIRK	KAREN	KYLE
LISA	LEE	LESLIE	LORENZO	LEAH
MARTIN	MARGOT	MILTON	MELISSA	MARCO
NICOLE	NIGEL	NADINE	NESTOR	NANA
OWEN	OPHELIA	OSCAR	OLGA	OMAR
PAULA	PHILIPPE	PATTY	PABLO	PAULETTE
RICHARD	RINA	RAFAEL	REBEKAH	RENE
SHARY	SEAN	SARA	SEBASTIEN	SALLY
TOBIAS	TAMMY	TONY	TANYA	TEDDY
VIRGINIE	VINCE	VALERIE	VAN	VICKY
WALTER	WHITNEY	WILLIAM	WENDY	WILFRED

WHIRLWIND FACT

The World Meteorological Organization keeps alphabetical lists of names for hurricanes. Names of major hurricanes are retired and not used again.

HOW DOES A HURRICANE FORM?

A hurricane begins with warm ocean water in the tropics.

The water heats the air above it. The air cools and forms clouds.

Steady winds push the clouds together.

The storm begins to **revolve**. The wind steers it across the ocean.

Formation of a Hurricane

eye

clouds form a storm system

rising warm air

wind

warm ocean air

WHIRLWIND FACT

Most hurricanes form between June 1st and November 30th. But they can happen any time of the year.

WHAT IS THE EYE OF A HURRICANE?

The eye is the center of the hurricane.

The hurricane **rotates** around the eye. The eye is usually 12 to 30 miles (20 to 50 kilometers) wide.

The eye is the calmest part of the storm. It has light winds.

Eyewall of Hurricane Katrina

WHIRLWIND FACT

The eyewall is the area just outside the hurricane's eye. The eyewall to the right of the eye is often the most destructive part of the storm.

TROPICAL DEPRESSIONS, TROPICAL STORMS, AND HURRICANES: WHAT'S THE DIFFERENCE?

All three are revolving storms. The difference is in the wind speed.

A tropical depression has steady winds that blow less than 39 miles (63 kilometers) per hour.

It becomes a tropical storm if winds reach a steady 39 miles (63 kilometers) per hour.

It's called a hurricane if it has **sustained** winds of 74 miles (119 kilometers) per hour.

WHIRLWIND FACT

Sometimes, hurricanes are called tropical cyclones or typhoons. They are all the same kind of storm.

WHY IS A HURRICANE DANGEROUS?

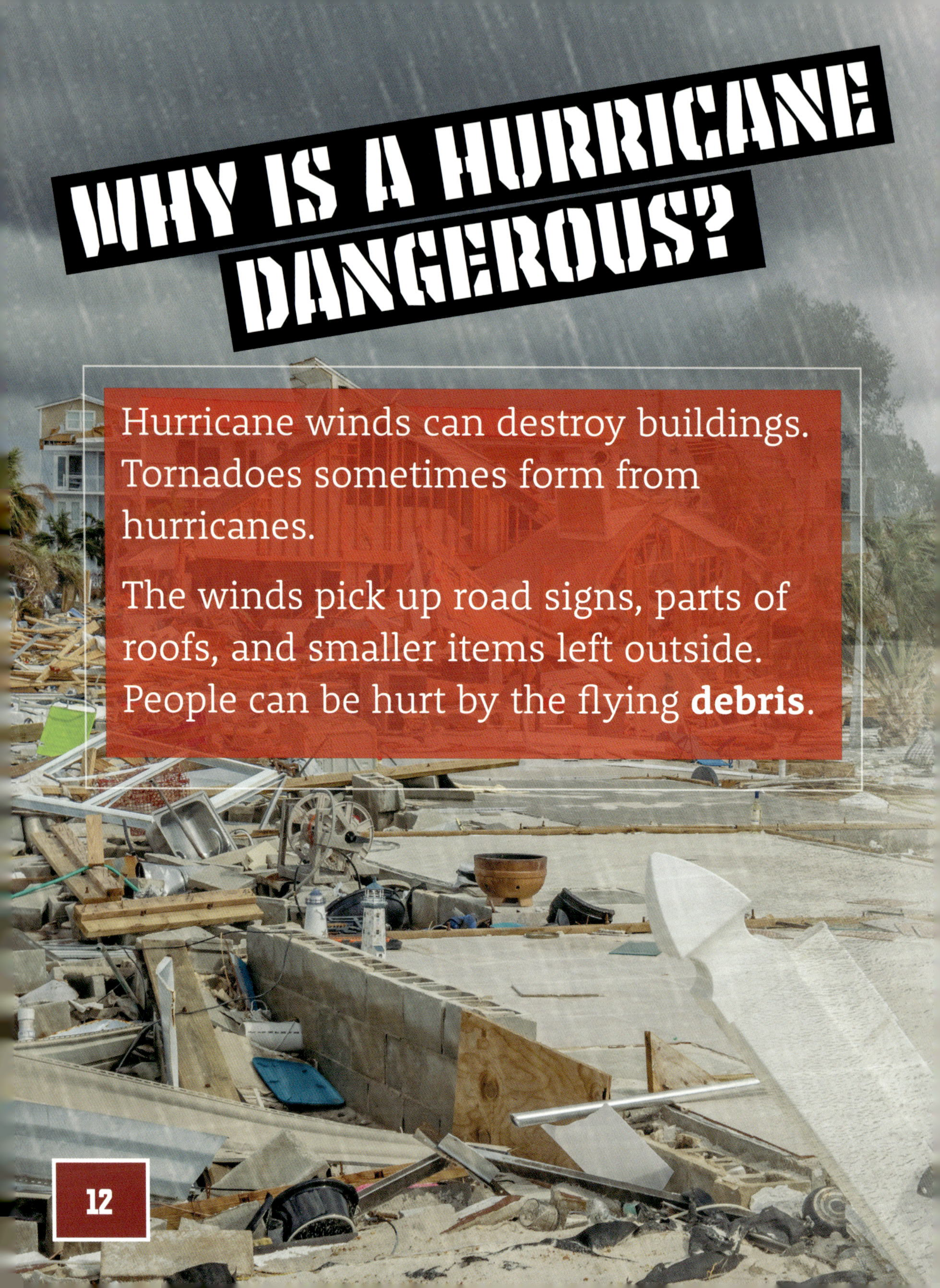

Hurricane winds can destroy buildings. Tornadoes sometimes form from hurricanes.

The winds pick up road signs, parts of roofs, and smaller items left outside. People can be hurt by the flying **debris**.

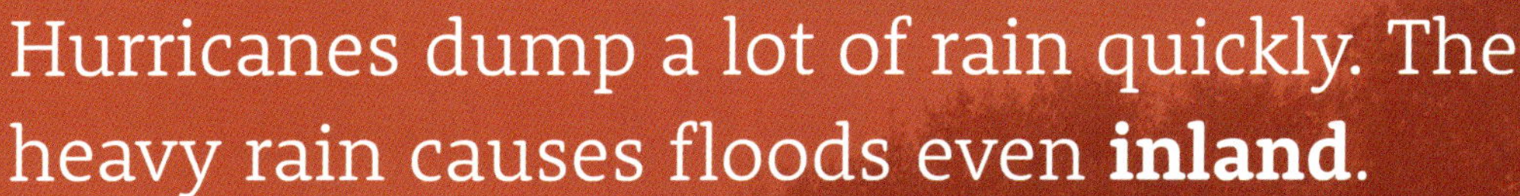

Hurricanes dump a lot of rain quickly. The heavy rain causes floods even **inland**.

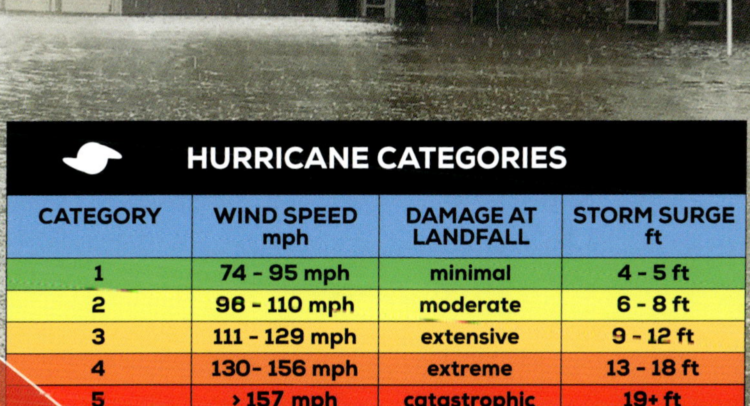

HURRICANE CATEGORIES

CATEGORY	WIND SPEED mph	DAMAGE AT LANDFALL	STORM SURGE ft
1	74 - 95 mph	minimal	4 - 5 ft
2	96 - 110 mph	moderate	6 - 8 ft
3	111 - 129 mph	extensive	9 - 12 ft
4	130- 156 mph	extreme	13 - 18 ft
5	> 157 mph	catastrophic	19+ ft

WHIRLWIND FACT

Hurricanes are rated on a wind scale from 1 to 5. A Category 1 is a minor hurricane that won't cause much damage. A Category 5 could flatten entire towns.

WHAT IS STORM SURGE?

Storm surge is the rise of ocean water above normal levels.

It happens where hurricane winds blow onshore.

A storm surge can increase the water level by 20 feet (six meters) or more.

It can **devastate** anything in its path.

Hurricane Ike-2008
Pensacola, Florida

Hurricane Sandy-2012
Seaside Heights, New Jersey

THE WORLD'S DEADLIEST HURRICANE

The Great Hurricane of 1780 hit the Caribbean islands before storm-tracking technology existed.

The winds destroyed even heavy stone buildings and forts.

More than 20,000 people died.

WHIRLWIND FACT

The Galveston Hurricane of 1900 was one of the deadliest in the United States. Up to 12,000 people died when the city of Galveston, Texas, was nearly destroyed.

PREDICTING A HURRICANE

Weather satellites and **radar** track tropical storms that form over the ocean.

Computers help analyze the information.

Forecasters decide when a tropical storm has become a hurricane.

They send out warnings online, on TV, and on the radio.

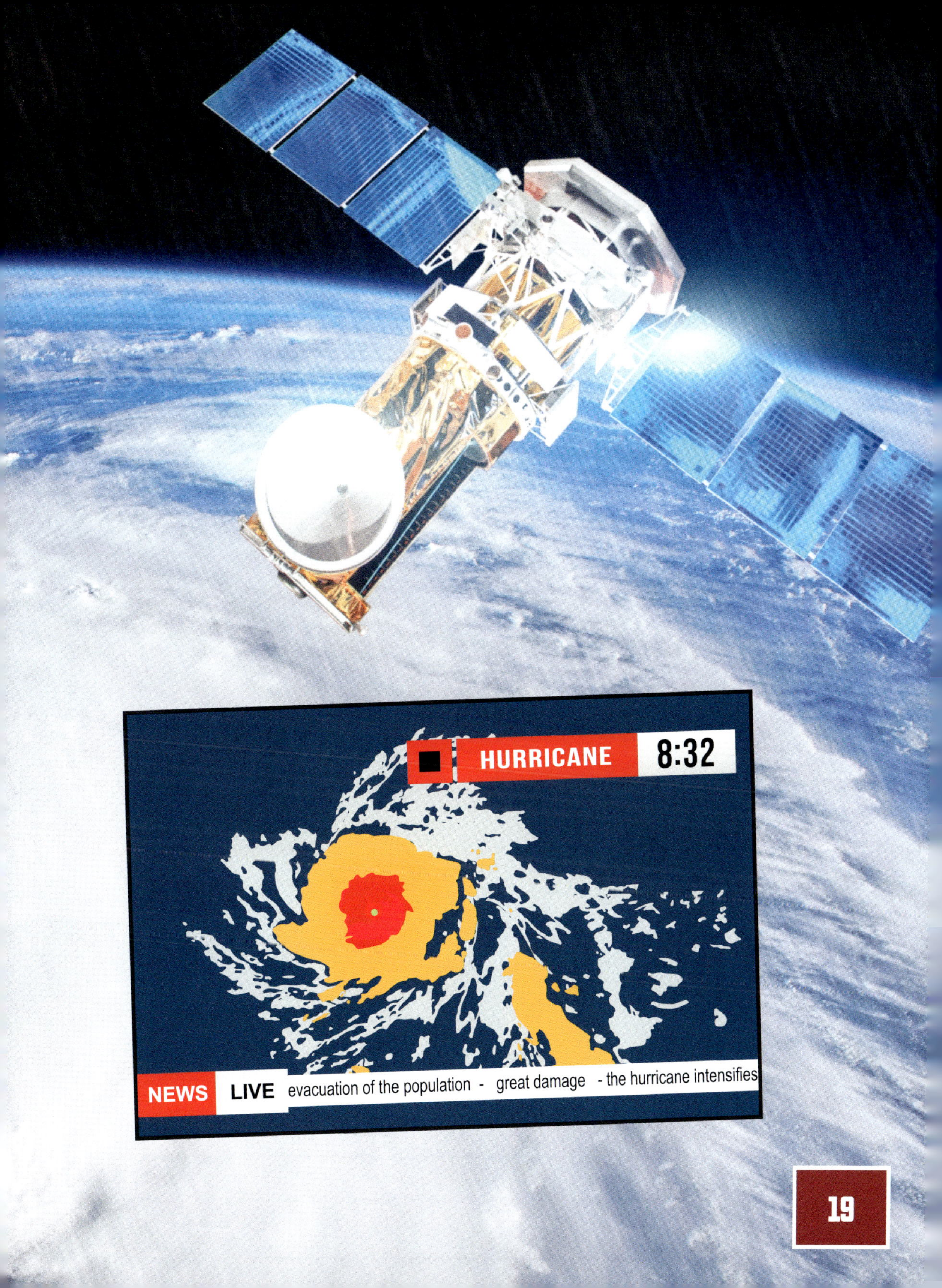

HURRICANE
8:32
NEWS
LIVE
evacuation of the population - great damage - the hurricane intensifies

STAYING SAFE DURING A HURRICANE

Make an emergency kit with water, food, and flashlights. Adults can cover windows with wood and bring outside furniture indoors.

Evacuate immediately if told to do so.

Go to a room without windows or a closet on the lowest floor if you shelter in place.

Do not go outside until the hurricane has completely passed.

GLOSSARY

debris (duh-BREE): remains or pieces of something broken down or destroyed

devastate (DEV-uh-stayt): to ruin or destroy

evacuate (i-VAK-yoo-ate): to move from a dangerous place to somewhere safer

inland (IN-luhnd): parts of a country away from the ocean

radar (RAY-dahr): a way to find things by reflecting radio waves off them and receiving the reflected waves; *radar* is an abbreviation for radio detection and ranging

revolve (ri-VAHLV): to turn around a center point

rotates (ROH-taytz): moves or turns in a circle

sustained (suh-STAYND): continuing for an extended period of time without stopping

WELCOME TO OIL PAINTING!

Oil painting has been around for centuries. In Europe, the technique has been used since about the eleventh century, and seventh-century cave paintings that used oil as a medium have been discovered in Bamiyan, Afghanistan. The practice of oil painting on a panel at an easel began to gain popularity in the fifteenth century. In those days, artists and their apprentices would mix their own oil colors by combining ground mineral pigments with some kind of plant-based oil, typically linseed oil. In 1841, portrait painter John Goffe Rand came up with a method of putting oil paint in zinc tubes, thereby paving the way for the convenience we modern painters enjoy.

Oil painting has been around for a long time, and there are as many ways to go about it as there are painters. I began to paint seriously in 1986 when I was in college and I have been painting just about every day for the past fifteen years. I've had a lot of time to figure out what the essential ingredients to a studio are. You don't need a ton of space or the fanciest tools. I'm going to go over what I feel are the basic necessities to get started in the fascinating world of oil painting.

BASIC TOOLS AND MATERIALS

Oil paint comes in student and professional grades. Professional-grade oil paint can be quite expensive, but in my experience, it's well worth the cost. It has a higher concentration and better quality of pigment than student-grade paint, and it is simply a joy to use. There are dozens of quality paint brands on the market, and the prices can vary quite a bit even among the professional grades. It's worth doing a bit of shopping around at first to find paint that you like and that is still reasonably affordable. It's not necessary that you stay loyal to a single brand. I have colors from half a dozen different makers in my paint box, and they all work quite well together.

For this book, I will be using a split primary palette. That is to say that I will have a warm and a cool version of each of the primary colors—red, yellow and blue. That is also to say that we will be using a limited palette with only a few base colors needed.

The specific paint that I will be using is Lukas 1862. Lukas 1862 is a professional-grade oil paint that is very vibrant and dries relatively quickly. It is readily available online and shouldn't break the bank. Winsor & Newton and Gamblin are two other brands that are of great quality and readily available from most art supply retailers. Here are the colors we will be using in this book:

- Alizarin crimson
- Cadmium red light
- Cobalt blue
- Cerulean blue
- Cadmium yellow lemon, called cadmium yellow light in most other brands
- Cadmium yellow, called cadmium yellow medium in most other brands
- Titanium white
- Ivory black

Something to Paint On

I prefer gessoed Masonite panels, but canvas board, primed chipboard or cardboard, oil paper and wood will all work just fine. Different substrates have different qualities—some are more textured or absorbent than others. You will need to do some experimenting to find out what works best for you. If you're going to paint every day, or close to it, you're going to need A LOT of panels. Cheap and plentiful are some great qualities of panels.

I purchase unprimed Masonite, known generically as hardboard, from my local lumberyard and then prime and cut it myself. However, if you don't have access to a table saw, this won't be possible. Jerry's Artarama (jerrysartarama.com) is a great source for all kinds of painting substrates. They have a wonderful selection of canvas board and gesso board panels in a variety of sizes, and they offer discounts if you buy in bulk. For the sake of keeping things simple, every project in this book is done on a 5 x 7–inch (13 x 18–cm) gesso board panel.

Something to Paint With

There are many different types of brushes and even more manufacturers. Generally, brushes are made with either bristle or hair. Bristle brushes are most commonly made from hog bristle and are stiffer than brushes made from the hair of other animals. They are ideal for pushing paint into the texture of your painting surface. Hair brushes are usually made from the hair of sable, weasel, squirrel or some other small animal. These are softer and are more appropriate for laying color down on top of wet paint if you don't want to disturb the previous layer. There are also some modern synthetics that work quite well for both of these applications.

Most of the projects in this book can be done with only two brushes. I use a small synthetic round brush for my initial drawing and for painting small areas and a ½-inch (1.3-cm) synthetic flat brush for just about everything else. In a pinch, the ½-inch (1.3-cm) flat brush would work for everything. Brush makers number their brushes to denote size, but there is no consistency in these size numbers across manufacturers. If the flat looks like it's about ½ inch (1.3 cm) wide, it will suffice. Brushes can be a very personal choice, and I suggest you try lots of different sizes, shapes and makes to find out what you prefer.

Something to Mix Paint On

Your palette is where you will put your paint. A flat surface works best for mixing colors with a palette knife (read more on that next). I use a large piece of ¼-inch (6-mm) tempered glass backed with a sheet of white foam core. The white background allows me to see and compare colors clearly, and the hard, smooth surface makes it easy to clean with a razor scraper even after the paint is dry. Disposable paper palettes that can be discarded after each painting session are also available.

Something to Mix Paint With

Palette knives are used to mix paint on your palette. If you use your brushes to do this, you will find that they don't last very long. Palette knives can also be used to apply paint to your painting or to scrape it off should you have the need. They are wonderful tools capable of both sharpening or softening edges in a painting (read more about that on page 21).

Something to Clean Your Brushes In

This can be as simple as an old soup can with some odorless mineral spirits in it, but I would suggest you get something designed for the task. A good brush cleaner should have a sieve that sits inside of it to make sure that your brushes stay out of the paint sediment that will accumulate at the bottom. It should also have a lid with a gasket so that you can travel safely with it. A lid is also handy for keeping fumes from escaping when it's not in use. In this book, I will sometimes refer to "mineral spirits" as "thinner." In addition to being used for cleaning brushes, I also use it for thinning my paint when I do my initial layout at the beginning of each painting.

You will also need some paper towels or clean cotton rags—old T-shirts work well. You will need these for cleaning your brushes and knives during your painting session. It is especially important that you get any excess thinner out of your brushes before you use them. Even a little bit of thinner in your paint can create a huge mess. Take my word on this.

Side Note: For the projects in this book, we will be mixing mineral spirits to thin the paint to block in the initial shapes at the beginning of each project. Just a bit of mineral spirits mixed with whatever paint color I recommend will do the trick.

Some Handy Extras

A short ruler is very valuable for ruling out *x* and *y* axes to help block in your subject when you are getting started on a painting. I use this to help me place the object on the panel and to aid in judging angles when I'm doing the initial layout.

A color isolator is a white or gray card with a hole punched in it. By holding it at arm's length and looking at various parts of your reference through the hole, you can isolate the various colors that you see. Taking a color out of context and surrounding it with white or gray often makes the color easier to see.

Mild dishwashing soap is great for cleaning your brushes. Use warm water with a little dishwashing soap at the end of each painting session after you clean them thoroughly in your brush cleaner. Your brushes will thank you.

Your stage has only three requirements: a flat stage to place your reference object on, a plain backdrop for it to show up against and a light source. I built a simple stage and backdrop years ago, and I eventually added walls and a ceiling to help isolate my stage lighting. I cut holes in the walls and top so I could move my light to a variety of places. In the past, I have used cardboard boxes with the front cut out, books leaned against each other or simply a table pushed up against a wall.

To the left is the current stage that I'm using. Right now, it has a piece of canvas draped in the background, and the light is an inexpensive clamp-on work light that is available at most hardware stores. For these projects, you will use my staged reference photos to paint our subjects. But if you want to paint subjects beyond this book, the above method is a simple way to stage whatever object it is that you want to paint.

LET'S SET UP A STUDIO!

Over the years, I have painted in a variety of spaces, including my kitchen, a spare bedroom, my garage, an old carriage house, a decaying shed and any number of classrooms. Several years ago, I tore down the decaying shed and built a studio in its place. This is the first time that I've had a place to paint that was specifically designed for the purpose. It is a wonderful luxury, but certainly not a necessity. At its most basic, all you need is a place to work and a place to put your reference subject.

A kitchen table or similarly sized work surface is a great place to start. Sit at one side and put your stage on the other. You don't want to have to move too much to look at your subject. For your panel, a small tabletop easel works great, but I typically just put my panel flat on the table surface. My stool is tall enough that I can look straight down at my painting and therefore avoid any distortions in the drawing. You will want enough surface space to accommodate your palette, brush cleaner and other tools.

THE PAINTING PROCESS

Describing an object with paint seems like a straightforward and simple task until you actually try it! The visual world is an incredibly busy place, and the amount of information that we receive through our eyes can be simply overwhelming. For this reason, we are going to try to isolate some visual ideas and work on them one at a time.

When you start to paint, it will be natural to wonder what to start with and how to proceed. I spent over twenty years teaching high school kids, most of whom had never held a paintbrush, intending to paint something realistically. Naturally, they would wonder what to do. This got me started on thinking about what I do when I paint. Every time I sat down to paint in my own studio, I would imagine myself describing the process to my students. Painting is such an interesting and complex activity. It starts in our heads when we see our subject, and then it comes out of our hands as we mix colors and apply them to a surface.

The Physical Process

This is the basic process that I go through when I paint: Once I have chosen a subject to paint, the very first thing I do is place it on my stage and arrange my lighting. For this book, you will use my photographs of our subjects as a reference, but if you want to stage your own subjects at home, you can. I typically light an object from the side so that the play of light across its surface creates an interesting interplay of light and dark areas that describe the form clearly and without confusion or ambiguity.

My stage is located right in front of me, 5 or 6 feet (1.5 or 1.75 m) in front of my painting table so I can easily look up and see it with minimum effort. I'm right-handed, so I place my palette to the right so that I can easily access it. I don't use an easel, so my painting panel is centered on the table directly in front of me. My paint, brushes, palette knives and brush cleaner are all easy for me to reach, and I make sure I have a clean rag or paper towels handy. When I'm in the studio, I'm always wearing clothes that I don't mind getting paint on.

Once I have my tools and supplies arranged, I observe my subject and block in the big shapes using oil paint mixed with a little bit of mineral spirits from my brush cleaner. The color that I use varies and is usually based on the colors that are in my subject. I don't put in a lot of detail here. I just want to get the main light and dark shapes placed on my panel. Once I have my subject blocked in, I mix all of the major color families that I'll be needing for the painting. I'm a big fan of premixing my colors, which you'll see in these projects. I've found that I can work more quickly and spontaneously if I don't have to stop to mix a new color group every time I get to a new portion of my painting. Once I have all the colors mixed, I generally start with the darkest colors first and start painting!

The Internal Process

The preceding section describes what I do when I am painting, but what am I thinking about? How do we decide where to put the paint to make a good or even readable painting? Over the years I gradually began to pare down the internal process to its bare essentials.

I came up with a flowchart (pictured on the next page) that sums it up nicely. The first step, doing something, could be choosing a material, mixing a color, making a mark or any one of a number of things that has to be done when you're starting a painting.

Let's say, for the purpose of our example, that you've made a mark. The next thing you'd do is to evaluate it. My high school kids would always get hung up on this step. They would say, "It's horrible!" and then throw it away! That's why I added the "be specific" note in parenthesis. If you're happy with your mark, you move up to the top of the chart and do the next thing, which is probably to make the next mark. If your mark needs work, you've got to figure out exactly what you don't like about it. Is it the wrong shape? Is it in the wrong place? Is it the wrong color? When you figure out the specific problem, it becomes relatively easy to address. Once you adjust it, you evaluate it again and either make further adjustments or move on. You will continue to make marks and adjust them as needed until the painting is finished.

THE WORK FLOW CHART

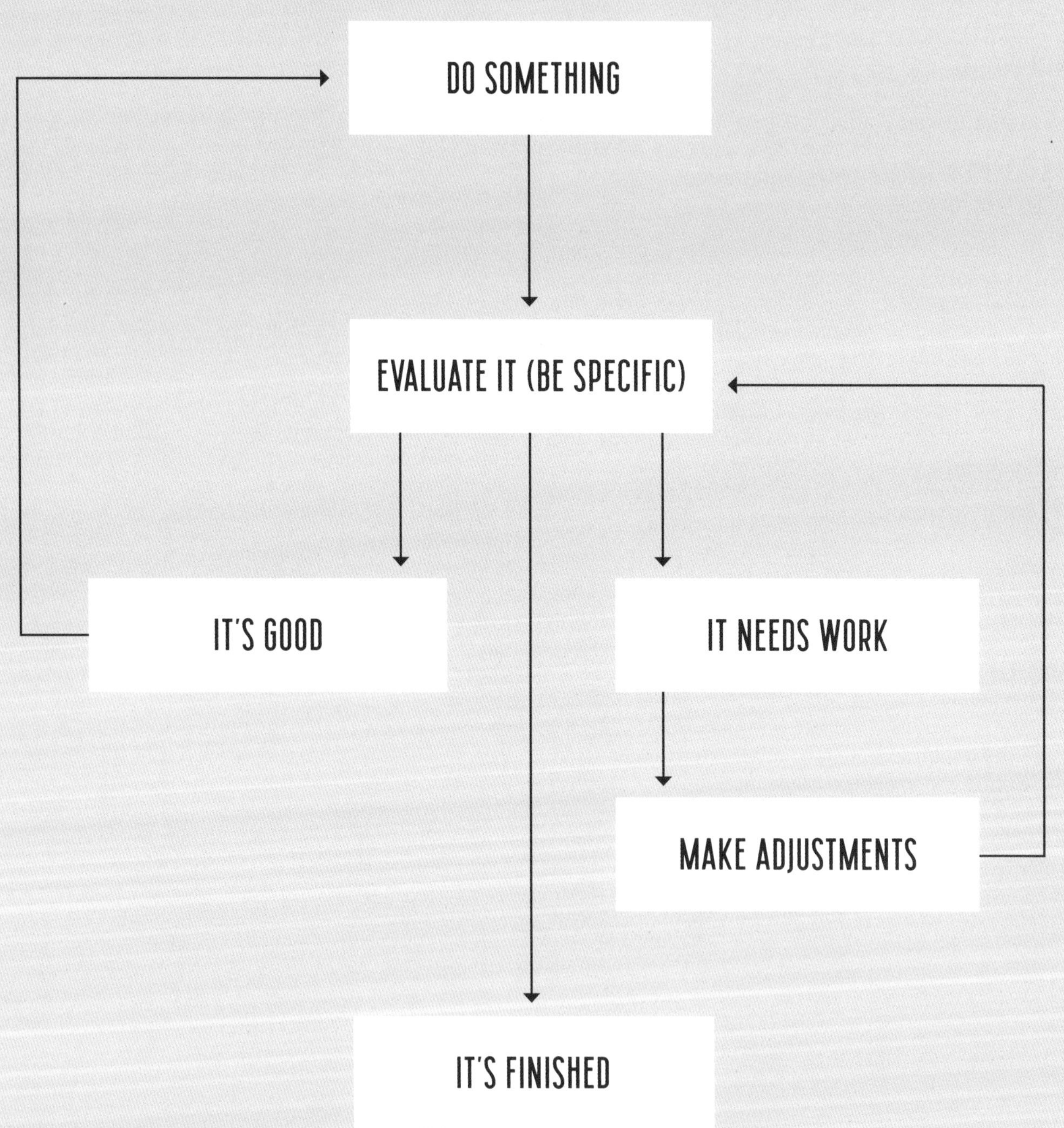

My students would often assume that the most important skill to learn was some kind of hand-eye, ninja-style coordination that you had to be born with. It's not. If you can write your name, you have all the manual dexterity you need to paint anything you want!

Assessing the problem is the thing that takes the most practice. As an art teacher, the question I get asked the most by far is some iteration of "What's wrong with this?" Giving an answer to that question too many times stunts the growth of that student. The ability to judge precisely what needs adjustment in a painting is exactly the skill that has to be developed to paint well. Painters who have a lot of practice move through the loops of the flowchart very quickly. Their actions are often in line with their intentions, so they spend a lot of time in the loop on the left, moving from one thing to the next relatively rapidly. When something does require adjustment, an experienced painter will have a good idea of what has to happen and will usually move through the right loop fairly quickly. If you're a beginner painter, it will look like the practiced painter is just making mark after mark that miraculously combine to create an illusion of depth and volume. What we can't see is the judgment that is behind each action.

THE LANGUAGE OF LIGHT

The way light plays across an object helps describe the form so that the resulting elements are predictable and consistent. Obviously, some forms are much more complex than others, but they still play by the same rules, and with a little practice, these elements will be recognizable to a greater or lesser extent in whatever you are painting. Throughout these projects, I will be describing how light affects our view of an object. Here are some quick definitions of those phrases so we are all on the same page.

Highlight(s): The area(s) of the object that is/are being hit by the most direct light.

Terminator: This is the edge that differentiates the lit side of an object from the shaded side. This edge will be more or less diffused depending on the composition of the object and the brightness of the light.

Reflected Light: This is the area on the shaded side of an object that is facing or partially facing the stage. Light reflects off of the stage and strikes this surface, creating a slightly lighter value than the core shadow.

Core Shadow: Core shadows appear where the surface of the object is parallel to the direction of both the direct light and the reflected light. These areas are often perpendicular to the horizontal stage. Since this area isn't being struck by either light source, it will have the darkest shadow on the surface of the object.

Cast Shadow: This is where the object blocks the light source from hitting the stage and creates a shadow.

Occlusion Shadow: The area where a form meets the stage or another form. It typically has a very dark shadow because so little light manages to get to this point of contact.

GETTING TO KNOW YOUR COLORS

There are four properties of color that I will be talking about throughout this book. They are hue, vibrancy, temperature and value. Here are some quick definitions of each one and what they mean for us as painters.

Hue: This refers to the color information. It sometimes seems almost too obvious to mention, but orange is a property of orange! This can be a very useful idea when we are trying to match a neutral tone that isn't clearly one of the primary (red, yellow and blue) or secondary (green, orange and violet) colors. If we have some idea of what to start with, it can make the job of mixing much easier.

Vibrancy: This refers to how pure a color is. The purer the color, the richer and more intense it is. Neutral tones like brown and gray are the opposite of vibrant.

Temperature: This is a relative term that we can use to compare different colors within our paintings. Red is a warm color, but some reds are warmer than others, just as blue is a cool color, but some blues can vary in temperature when compared to other blues. Violet and green are both secondary colors that are made by combining a warm primary—red and yellow, respectively—with a cool primary such as blue. Red-violet is warm when compared to blue-violet but is cool when compared to pure red.

Value: It has been said that color gets all the credit while value does all the work. Value is the light or dark quality of a color. Imagine taking a black-and-white photograph of the color wheel. This is reducing the color wheel down to just value. Our eyes are very good at reading value. Black-and-white images are instantly recognizable. We don't need hue, value or temperature to know what's going on. Yellow is the pure hue with the lightest value, and violet is the darkest.

The Color Wheel

I think just about everyone is familiar with the basic color wheel. The visible light spectrum starts with red and ends in violet. These pure hues are, in order, red, orange, yellow, green, blue and violet. Infrared and ultraviolet are at the far ends of this spectrum and not visible to the human eye, so we will not worry about those. This spectrum then is wrapped around in a circle to make the color wheel. Once we match the two ends together, we end up with a fairly useful tool for understanding color.

Imagine slicing a circle into sixths and then placing the three primary colors into every other wedge. The blank slices between the primaries would each be filled in by the secondary color—orange, green or violet—that is created by mixing the colors that are adjacent to it. Between red and yellow, you would put orange; between yellow and blue would be green; and between blue and red would be violet.

Understanding Color Bias

So far, we have dealt with the visible spectrum of light, but since we are painting with pigment, not light, it is theoretical. We can't buy a tube of paint that is pure blue. We have to content ourselves with pigments found in the natural world, and it would be a very rare thing to find a shade of blue that was just blue with zero bias toward green or violet.

Color bias is the idea that whatever pigment of blue we find at the local art supply store will not be straight blue but will in fact be pushed slightly toward violet or slightly toward green. The same could be said for any primary color we can find on the market.

I chose the colors for the materials list in these projects with that in mind. You will notice that there are two versions of each primary. Each version is biased toward the secondary color on either side of it. We have:

- Cadmium red light (orange bias)
- Alizarin crimson (violet bias)
- Cadmium yellow lemon (green bias)
- Cadmium yellow (orange bias)
- Cerulean blue (green bias)
- Cobalt blue (violet bias)

One of our tasks as painters is to understand the colors we are using. To help with this, I'd like you to make a color bias color wheel. This exercise is extremely valuable because it starts to give you an idea of the various colors that are possible with your palette. It will look something like the image to the left.

Here's what I did to make mine: I drew three concentric circles to make two rings. The circles are just to help us organize the colors, with the outer ring for pure hues and the inner ring for those same hues tinted with white. This helps to see the hues more easily, especially those that have dark values. I then divided each circle into sixths. Notice that the portions I've placed my primaries in have each been divided in half. This is so I can put both versions of each primary next to each other.

I've put each primary on the side that it's biased toward. In other words, cerulean blue is on the green side and cobalt blue is on the violet side. I then mixed each secondary color—orange, green and violet—with the primary adjacent to it whose bias will create the most vibrant version of that secondary color. For example, cadmium red light and cadmium yellow for orange, cerulean blue and cadmium yellow lemon for green and cobalt blue and alizarin crimson for violet. I filled in this entire secondary segment of the outer ring with that color.

You will notice three tabs overlaid on the secondary segments. These are secondary colors mixed with the primaries that are the opposite of their bias. The orange tab is mixed with alizarin crimson and cadmium yellow lemon, the green tab is mixed with cobalt blue and cadmium yellow and the violet tab is mixed with cerulean blue and cadmium red light. You can see that those secondaries are much more muted than our previous secondary mixtures.

To the left, you'll see that I took a couple of pieces of Arches oil paper and made 5 x 6–inch (13 x 15–cm) grids on them. Primary colors go on the left and secondaries go on the right. For these, I used the vibrant secondaries that I mixed on the bias for the previous color wheel exercise. The top row of each card is the red/green pair. The primary and secondary colors, or pure hues, go in the squares at the end of each row. The middle square of each row is as neutral as I can get it by mixing each complementary pair together. The squares on either side are versions of the pure hues that have been slightly desaturated by their complement. Each pair is followed by a version that has been tinted with white. You could also make another set using the muted secondary colors from the tabs that were mixed off of the bias. The more you do, the better grasp you will have of what your palette is capable of.

Again, the purpose of these exercises is to give you an idea of what is possible. I keep mine close at hand to use as a reference when I'm trying to figure out where to start with a color that's difficult to figure out.

Complementary Pairs

Colors that are opposite each other are called complementary pairs. They would be red and green, blue and orange, and yellow and violet. Complementary pairs neutralize each other when they are mixed together. This is a very useful thing in painting that helps us control the vibrancy of a color. I've put together a couple of other quick exercises that you can do to help you further understand the range of colors achievable with what you have.

Understanding Color Relationships

When we paint, we must strive to make each color relate to its adjacent colors properly. Because the colors in a painting do not exist in isolation, the interaction of colors is more important to consider than each individual color. As hard as we may try to match the actual colors of the real world, we are destined to fail. For example, the play of light across a reflective surface is likely to shine directly in our eyes at some point. This will appear as a very bright, light-value area in our reference. Depending on the intensity of the light source, it may even cause us to squint. In our painting, we will not have the advantage of being able to shine a light in our viewer's eyes. We must instead create a set of relationships that makes white paint look like the light reflecting in the viewer's eyes.

A color surrounded by a darker color will look lighter than it would if it were surrounded by a lighter color.

Colors look more intense when they are compared to neutral tones than when they are surrounded by more vibrant colors. Throughout this book, I will be talking about "color relationships." You will often hear me say "let's check our color relationships" in our projects. More or less, this will mean checking how our colors look together in a painting and if the colors painted side by side complement each other in a way that accurately captures the color we see in real life. These relationships can also be thought of as types of contrast. Where we have contrast, we have edges. We can contrast any one of the properties of color: hue, vibrancy, temperature or value. Some passages may have contrast in all four. In general, our eyes will be drawn to areas of greater contrast, while areas of low contrast will tend to recede into the background. It is our task to take advantage of these concepts to create a set of color relationships that best expresses what we see.

Speaking of Edges

An edge is any place where two tones meet. Edges can be sharp or soft. Some edges are so soft that they vanish altogether and become vanishing or implied edges. Painters use the quality of their edges to lead the viewer's eye through a painting.

Lower-contrast edges are naturally softer than higher-contrast edges. Throughout this book, you will hear me say "let's soften our edges." There are a number of ways to soften an edge. Paint can be physically dragged from one area to another on the painting with a brush, knife, finger, rag or whatever else is handy. Adding an intermediate tone between two adjacent colors is another effective way to soften an edge. When I refer to an "internal edge," I'm talking about a tonal shift that takes place within the form or subject and isn't a part of the perimeter's edge. Sometimes these are very soft—think of the transitions that you would see on a peach or tennis ball. Sometimes these internal edges can be quite sharp and high contrast, like what you would see in a reflective, metallic surface.

Whatever the case, edge quality is a powerful tool for differentiating textures and materials as well as getting your objects to look like they are a part of their environment.

USING VALUE TO DESCRIBE FORM

Value refers to the light or dark quality of a color. Of all the properties of color, it is the most important to get right. Our eyes are capable of recognizing an image using only value. This is why black-and-white photographs are so easily readable. This is an amazing and wonderful ability that the human eye possesses. The downside is that if we get the values wrong, we will create an image that may be confusing or unrecognizable.

Light and shadow are most easily described in terms of value, and if we eliminate hue, vibrancy and temperature, we can more easily concentrate on and appreciate the power of value. I often do a quick value study when I am trying to understand a complicated color relationship. The projects in this chapter will demonstrate how value affects a painting, which is a good foundation to start with before we start adding in an array of colors.

GRAYSCALE SPHERE

Painting in grayscale allows us to isolate value. The lack of color rarely hinders our ability to recognize what we are looking at. A sphere is a wonderful form to paint. It's very simple, but it contains all of the things that we will be concerning ourselves with throughout this book. I'll be using a 4-inch (10-cm) Styrofoam™ ball that I coated with white gesso.

What You'll Need

Panel
Paints: ivory black, titanium white
Palette
Palette knife
Brushes
Brush cleaner
Mineral spirits
Paper towels or cloth rags
Ruler

What Do We See?

Our sphere is lit from the upper left and is roughly divided in half, giving us a lit side and a shaded side. In this case, the edge that is closest to the light source is the lightest value, and we have a series of light halftones leading us to the terminator. The terminator is where the lit side transitions to shadow. The shaded side is made up of the core shadow and reflected light. The other major element that we can see is the cast shadow. You will notice that the cast shadow isn't a constant value. There is light bouncing off of the sphere and the backdrop, which creates some interesting value shifts within the cast shadow. The darkest area of the cast shadow is the occlusion shadow. This is the area directly beneath the form where the most light is blocked. This is usually the darkest value in the composition.

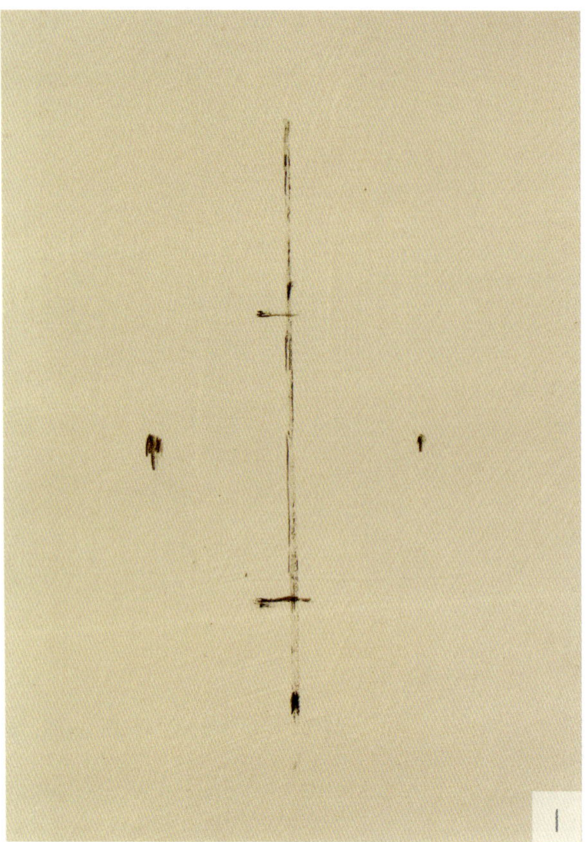

1

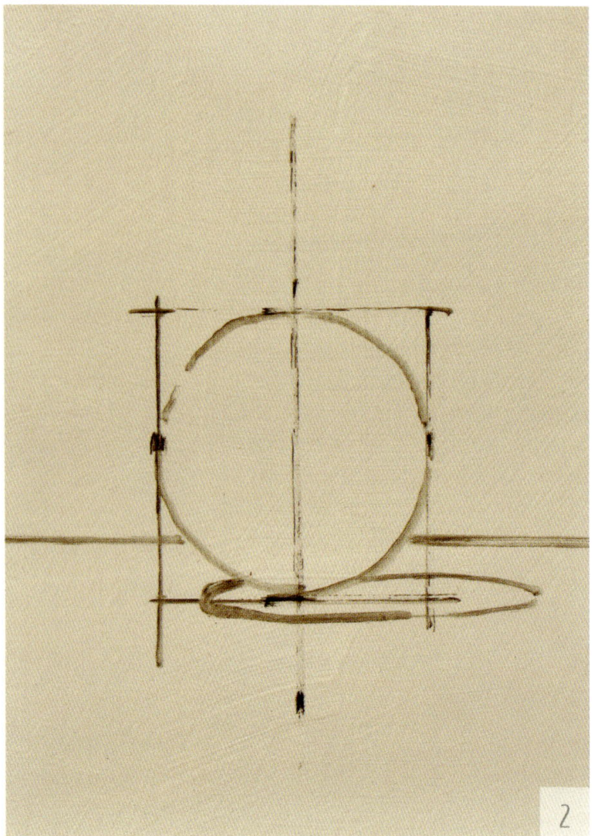

2

Blocking In Your Subject

1. I start by mixing a little bit of mineral spirits from my brush cleaner with my ivory black paint. The trick is to get it to flow like ink. If you add too much thinner, it will bleed and be hard to control. I then draw a vertical line in the center and make a few marks to indicate its height and width.

2. A circle is as tall as it is wide, so drawing a square first can be a good way to accurately make this shape. I also include the outline of the cast shadow. This ellipse will flatten the closer your stage is to your eye level. Once I have the basic shapes down, I'm ready to mix some values.

Mixing Your Colors

3. Using my ivory black and titanium white paint, I mix five shades of gray. If I include my unmixed ivory black and titanium white, I will have a total of seven values to work with. The darkest gray will be for the occlusion shadow, the next darkest will be the core shadowing and the middle gray will be for the reflected light. My remaining light grays will be the halftones that, combined with white, will make up the light side of our sphere as well as the bulk of the background.

3

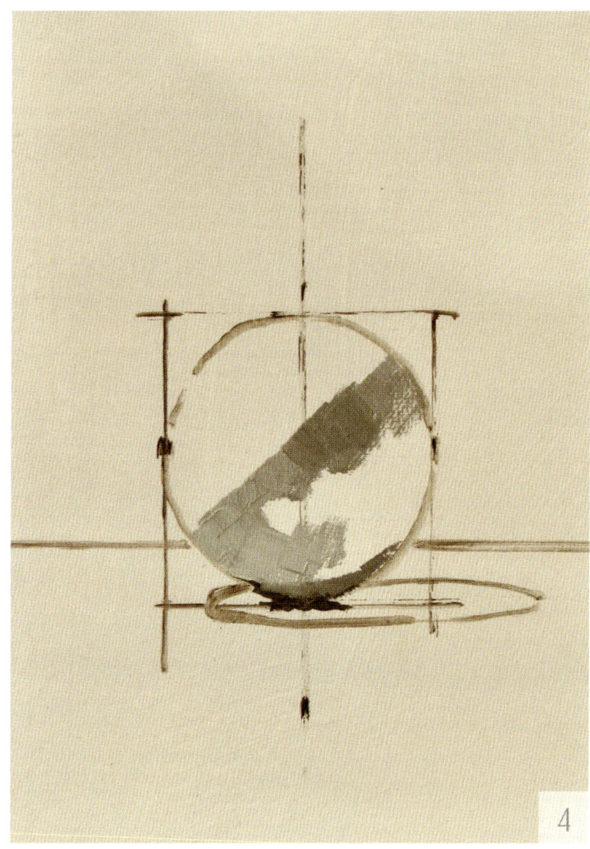
4

Painting

4. Once our values are mixed, we're ready to start painting. I start with the darkest value at the bottom of the sphere and then move on to the next darkest in the core shadow. Once these are established, I start to link them together with the next darkest value, the reflected light. I generally work from dark to light. Dark colors show up better on a white panel, so they're easier to see initially. Also, light colors typically have more white in them and are more opaque, making them easier to lay over darker, more transparent pigments.

5. Once I establish the reflected light, I move to the lighter colors that comprise the halftones on the lit side of the subject. These same tones also occur in the background behind the dark side of the sphere, so I block in some background color as well to make sure that relationship is sound.

6. I continue adding the halftones on the lit side as I bring the background all the way around the object. Notice that the sphere is darker than the background on its dark, bottom side and lighter than the background on the lit, upper side. There are even some small areas where the tones are identical and the edge disappears entirely. Accurately seeing these relationships is a big part of creating a convincing illusion.

7. Using the same values that I used for the core shadow and the reflected light, I block in the cast shadow. The back edge of the cast shadow is a little lighter because the backdrop of the stage is reflecting a lot of light back into it. Cast shadows also typically get lighter the farther away they are from the object casting them. The stage surface is a little lighter than the vertical backdrop because it is being struck by the light more directly. When I'm doing simple studies like this, I will often just surround the object with some background and foreground color so that it has an environment to sit in and call it a day. I don't always find it necessary to paint all the way to the edge of my panel or sketchbook page. As William Merritt Chase said, "It takes two to paint. One to paint, the other to stand by with an axe to kill him before he spoils it."

VALUE STUDY: BLACK CUBE

Painting a black object is an interesting endeavor. The entire cube is black. That is to say, I made a cube out of wood and painted it with black paint. I know that the local color is black on all six sides. In art, "local color" refers to the natural color of an object or part of an object. The fascinating thing is that we will only be using pure black paint in very select parts of our painting. Where light is striking the cube more directly, the value is quite a bit lighter than black. This is a great exercise for comparing values.

What You'll Need

Panel

Paints: ivory black, titanium white

Palette

Palette knife

Brushes

Brush cleaner

Mineral spirits

Paper towels or cloth rags

Ruler

What Do We See?

At most, we can only see three sides of a cube at one time. I've set my subject up with a slightly elevated vantage point so that we can see the top and two sides. The cube I'm using is a bit worn from use, but it will do for our purpose. I'm going to ignore the imperfections and concentrate on the big picture. The left vertical face of the cube is the darkest overall. The top plane is the lightest value because the light is striking it most directly. And the right vertical face has the most variation due to the light reflecting onto it from the side wall of my stage. The bottom of this plane is close to the darkest value on the cube because the cast shadow reflects very little light up onto it.

STEPHENS
7·3·21

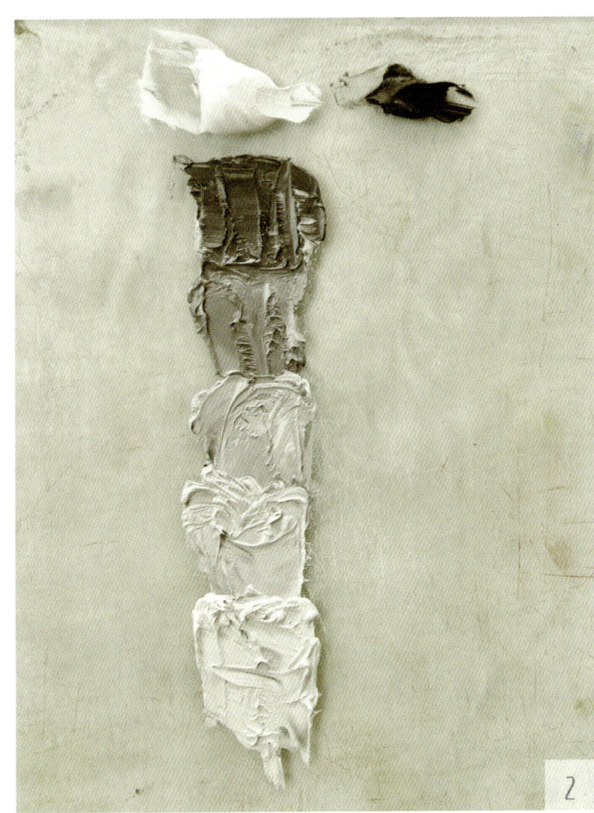

Blocking In Your Subject

1. I start by mixing a little bit of mineral spirits with ivory black paint. Using a brush, I then paint a vertical axis to hang my shapes on and to find the visual center of the form. When I block this in, I'm constantly comparing my angles to this vertical line. I'm not doing anything fancy here. I'm just eyeballing it and adjusting things until it looks right. I include some extra marks to differentiate some of the value variations in the cast shadow.

Mixing Your Colors

2. Using my ivory black and titanium white paints, I mix five shades of gray. With my ivory black and titanium white, I will have a total of seven values to work with. For the cube, I'll be using the two darkest grays and the pure black. The lighter grays will be used for the background, with the cast shadow falling in the mid-range of these values.

Painting

3. I start by blocking in everything that is pure black. That includes the top half of the left vertical plane and the bottom of the right vertical plane as well as its upper-right corner. There is also a thin occlusion shadow along the bottom edge of the left plane.

4. I fill in the rest of the left plane. It gets lighter as we move down, so I start with my darkest gray and then switch to the second darkest. I also block in some lighter gray, our third darkest value, where the two vertical planes meet. I am always comparing values where the planes come together. The amount of light striking any given plane is dependent on its relationship to the light source. It's important that the values in the painting support what I'm seeing in my reference. Keep in mind that all of this could be radically different depending on the lighting situation.

5. I finish roughing in the right plane and soften the internal edges. When I talk about "internal edges," I'm talking about the areas where there are tonal shifts within the cube, as opposed to the edges that differentiate the cube from the background. The sharpest edges will be around the perimeter and where the planes meet.

6. I block in the top plane, which is a relatively uniform mid-range value. I'm using the third, or middle mixed value for this. I also put in the part of the cast shadow that is the same value.

7. I block in the rest of the cast shadow and put some background and foreground color around the form. For the foreground, I'm using the very lightest mixed gray, and the background is one step darker than that. This is a good opportunity to check my value relationships.

8. I use a knife to adjust and straighten some of my edges and put in the white highlight where the top plane meets the vertical planes. I also take this opportunity to soften some of the areas within the planes where different values meet. On simple studies like this, I sometimes don't paint all the way to the edges of my panel. I just need enough background to be able to judge my value relationships.

Some Notes on Lighting Your Subject

When I set up an object on my stage, I am going for the view that describes it best. You will notice that all of these exercises are lit from the upper side. The reason that I prefer upper-side lighting is simply that it does the best job of describing the form. When objects are lit from the front, they tend to look flat and washed out. The lack of shadows playing across the surface can create ambiguous, low-contrast areas that make the form difficult to read, and the cast shadow, which can offer wonderful clues to the nature of a form, ends up being obscured by the object. When objects are lit from the upper side, we get the full range of light and shadow. The light halftones, core shadow, reflected light and cast shadow all work together to describe what we are painting.

VALUE STUDY: GRAY CYLINDER

We finish off our study of basic forms with a gray cylinder. I found a wooden one at a friend's house. It was part of a set of blocks belonging to her son. They were nice enough to give it to me, and I painted it medium gray. A toilet paper or paper towel tube would have worked just as well, but I liked how substantial the wooden one was.

What You'll Need

Panel

Paints: ivory black, titanium white

Palette

Palette knife

Brushes

Brush cleaner

Mineral spirits

Paper towels or cloth rags

Ruler

What Do We See?

The local color of our cylinder is medium gray, but it's a lot darker than that in the shadowed areas. The lightest part of our subject is the top elliptical plane because it is getting the most direct light. We can see a band of core shadow running down vertically from the top, which starts to wash out by the bottom third of our form because it's catching more reflected light from the stage. There is a fairly broad range of values going from nearly white to not quite black.

STEPHENS
7·2·21

1

2

Blocking In Your Subject

1. I mix a little bit of mineral spirits with ivory black and find the center of my panel. I make a vertical mark and use it to place the sides of my form. I then determine the height of the cylinder. My eye level is a little higher than the top of the cylinder, so there is a flattened ellipse at the top and bottom.

Mixing Your Colors

2. I start by mixing a dark gray from ivory black and titanium white that approximates the darkest value on the model. Then, I gradually add more titanium white until I have five values, with the lightest being equivalent to the lightest gray on my cylinder. I can always adjust these as needed once I start painting, but they should suffice.

3

4

5

Painting

3. I start with the darkest value in the core shadow and in the narrow occlusion shadow at the bottom.

4. I then move a step lighter and establish the reflected light along the right side and bottom of the form. I make sure to include the dark bit in the lower-right corner of the form where we can see the reflection of the cast shadow.

5. I move on to the halftones on the light side of the form. I'm using the third value from the lightest for this.

6. I then paint the light value on the top plane of the cylinder with the lightest gray on my palette. I also paint in the background so that I have something to compare my values to. For this, I use the value that is a step darker than what I used for the top of the cylinder.

7. To finish, I paint in the cast shadow and add the foreground color. The cast shadow is a combination of the second and third values from the lightest, and the foreground color is the lightest value that I have mixed. I also add some intermediate values to soften the transitions in the halftones on the lit side of the form. Additionally, I smooth out the distracting texture on the top elliptical plane.

Some Notes on Texture

One of the great things about oil paint is the physicality of the textures that it is capable of creating. Thickly painted passages are referred to as "impasto." You can use areas of impasto to emphasize passages or smooth the finish out if you want an area to be less of a focal point. Different tools create different types of textures. I am fond of palette knives because they can be used to both create and subdue texture. I try to avoid texture for its own sake. My goal is to have texture, or the lack thereof, support the overall idea of the painting.

VALUE STUDY: PEAR

We have made it through to our first organic form! Pears are a delight to paint. They all have a slightly different shape and yet they are all distinctly recognizable as pears. I like them because their form is a little bit more complex than an apple or an orange, which creates some interesting shadows across their surface. Pears have always seemed slightly anthropomorphic to me, imbuing them with a bit more personality than your average fruit basket citizen.

What You'll Need

- Panel
- Paints: ivory black, titanium white
- Palette
- Palette knife
- Brushes
- Brush cleaner
- Mineral spirits
- Paper towels or cloth rags
- Ruler

What Do We See?

One of the first things I noticed with this pear is its brilliant color. We are going to ignore that for now, though. Up until this point, we have been painting black-and-white objects with black and white paints. This time, we are going to have to isolate the value information in our heads. This is an important skill for a painter to learn. Our subject has slightly glossy skin, so it's a bit more reflective than the objects we've painted up until this point. That gloss causes it to pick up reflections more readily, and you might notice that the transitions between light and dark areas are a little more abrupt. Our light source is coming from the upper-right corner, and we can see that the lit side of the pear is a little bit lighter in value than the background. The lit side is made up of light halftones and a very distinct hotspot in the highlight. On the shaded side, the pear is clearly darker than the background. We still have a very distinct core shadow and reflected-light areas. The core shadow is long and narrow because of our eye level and the direction of the light source.

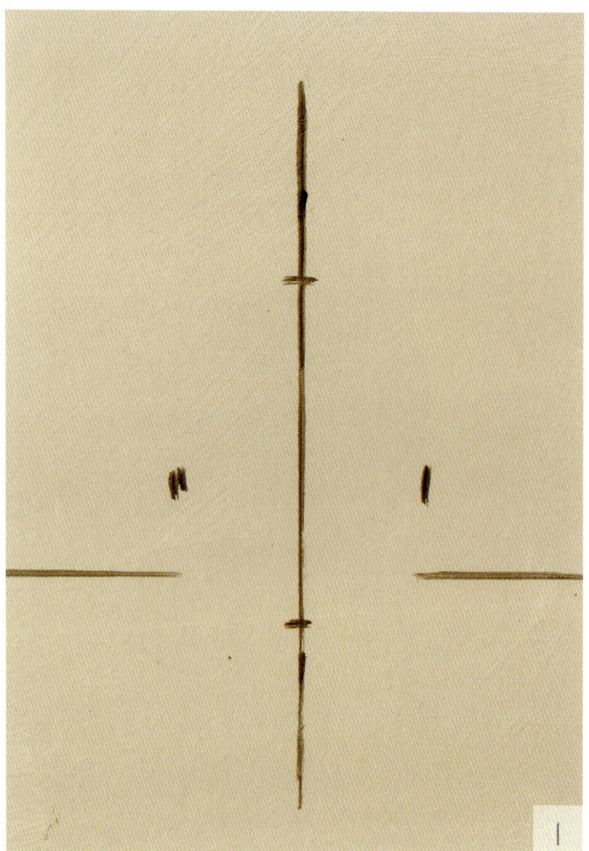

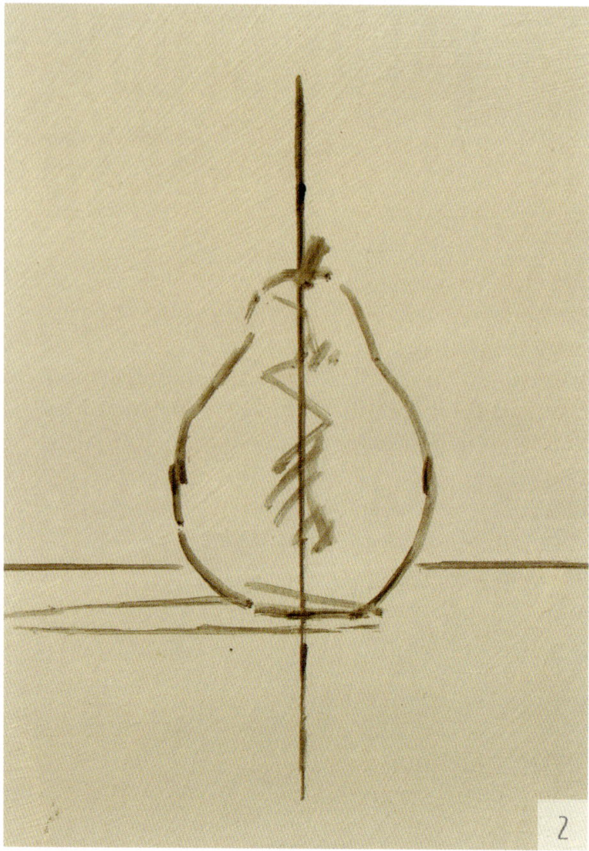

Blocking In Your Subject

1. Using our mixture of mineral spirits and ivory black paint, I draw a vertical line in the center and make a few marks to indicate its height and width.

2. Next, I rough in the silhouette of the pear as well as the basic shape of the cast shadow. I'm also including some marks to indicate where the core shadow will be.

Mixing Your Colors

3. Using my titanium white and ivory black paint, I mix five shades of gray. With the pure ivory black and titanium white, I will have a total of seven values to work with. The darkest gray will be for the occlusion shadow at the bottom of the pear, the next darkest will be the core shadowing and the middle gray will be for the reflected light. My remaining light grays will be the halftones that, combined with titanium white, will make up the light side of our pear as well as the bulk of the background.

Painting

4. I start by blocking in the darkest values in the stem and the occlusion shadow at the very bottom, and then I move on to the core shadow. Notice how the core shadow moves across the irregular surface of the pear.

5. Continuing from dark to light, I then establish the reflected light on the left side of the pear. At this point, I feel it's important to put in some background color so I can check the relationship between the reflected light and the ground. I use the second lightest mixed value for this.

6. Next, I continue to the lit side of the pear, establishing the light halftones. I continue blocking in the background to make sure my figure/background relationships are good. Generally, I want the pear to be darker than the background on the shadow side and lighter than the background on the lit side. There will probably be areas where the edge disappears entirely and that's okay.

7. Using the same values that occur in the core shadow and reflected light areas on the pear, I then block in the cast shadow. I use the lightest gray value to establish the foreground.

8. Finally, I paint in the rest of the background and foreground and smooth out some of my transitions. The last thing I do is add some highlights to the pear using pure white. They occur near the middle of the lightest area.

Some Notes on Practice

When I mentioned to a friend of mine that I was writing an instructional book on oil painting, he immediately asked me what I had to offer to the cumulative knowledge of Western art. I realized then and there that the answer was, nothing. I came close to giving up on the project in that moment, but then I realized that what I did have to offer was a method of practicing and gradually improving that might resonate with some people. My experience in teaching inexperienced teenagers had taught me that most people can learn to paint, and if they have the desire to improve, all they need is a little time and the impetus to get started. The best instructional book in the world will do you no good unless you get at it and start. Hopefully, the projects contained in these pages will help you get the ball rolling. Now that you've gotten some practice pushing paint around, let's continue on and see how we can build upon these new skills together!

GETTING A HANDLE ON COLOR TEMPERATURE

Temperature is an important property of color. It's more relative and subtle than value, and it can be an important tool in our quest to describe our world through oil paint. Red, orange and yellow are all warm hues. Blue is cool, and violet and green are often thought of as cool, especially when compared to the warmer colors. In general, warm colors come forward and cool colors tend to recede. Neutral tones can be warm or cool depending on what they are compared to. Brown and tan would be examples of warm neutrals, and gray would be an example of a cooler neutral. In this chapter, I'll be talking a little bit about "halftones". Halftones are halfway in tone between the darks and lights. They are typically found on the lit side of an object near the terminator where the lights are transitioning to dark. For these projects, we are going to see how we can use temperature to help us achieve the illusion of volume and space on a two-dimensional panel.

STEPHENS
4·27·21

ACCENTUATED PEAR

We've painted a pear in grayscale where we had the opportunity to isolate the form and just concentrate on value. Now, we're going to add that beautiful, warm green color to the equation. In color, temperature is relative. Green is a cool color when compared to red, yellow or orange, but it's warm when compared to blue and some violets. Within the family of colors that we would classify as "green," there are warmer and cooler versions. We're going to explore some of those ideas and see how they can help us describe light and form.

What You'll Need

Panel

Paints: cadmium red light, cadmium yellow lemon, cobalt blue, titanium white

Palette

Palette knife

Brushes

Brush cleaner

Mineral spirits

Paper towels or cloth rags

Ruler

What Do We See?

To me, the most striking thing about this pear is the vibrant yellow-green color. The lit side has a lot more yellow in it, and it's so warm that it makes our warm, neutral backdrop look a little cool. The core shadow is nice and distinct, and the reflected-light area, while still warm, is decidedly cooler than the lit side of our pear. The stem and occlusion shadow are the darkest elements of our tableau.

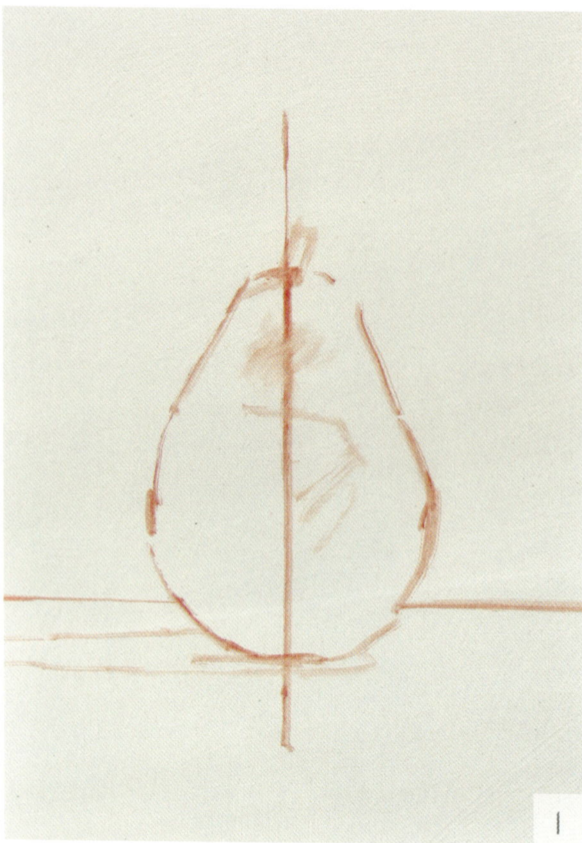

1

2

Blocking In Your Subject

1. I'm mixing a little bit of mineral spirits with a bit of cadmium red light because why not? Most of our lay-in will be covered in the end anyway. I'm starting with a vertical mark to help place my subject. Once I mark the overall height and width, I block in the big shapes. I'm shooting for something that is universally pear-like. My reference is there to guide me and help keep me from making any internal contradictions in my drawing, but I'm not interested in being controlled by it, and you shouldn't be either. I include a few marks to indicate the terminator, which is the soft edge separating the lit and shaded sides.

Mixing Your Colors

2. I start by mixing green with the cadmium yellow lemon and cobalt blue. I add a little more cobalt blue to the mix, moving from left to right. This cools down the mixture and makes the value a little darker. Finally, I add a touch of cadmium red light. This makes the green more neutral and darkens the value even more.

3. I add a little bit more cobalt blue to my green mixture and then a little titanium white to lighten the value. This will become my core shadow and reflected light. Next, I mix a warm yellow-green to the right. I want this to be clearly warmer than my previous green, so I start with some of the mid-range green that I just mixed and then add titanium white to it until the value is right. White tends to cool colors off and it also reduces the vibrancy, so I add some cadmium yellow lemon to this mixture to warm it back up and restore some of its punch. "Punch" is synonymous with vibrancy here!

4. The last color thread we need to mix is the background, foreground and cast shadow. I want the background to be clearly cooler than the pear, so I'm going to use violet as my starting point. I mix that with the only red and blue on my palette, which is cadmium red light and cobalt blue. I then add some titanium white. This both lightens the value and reduces the vibrancy of the color. Once I get the value of the background right—it should be a little darker than the lightest pear color—I can move on to the foreground. This will be the background color plus titanium white to lighten the value even more and just a touch of cadmium yellow lemon to warm it up ever so slightly. Finally, I take some of the original dark violet and add titanium white until I match the value of the cast shadow, and then I add a little bit of yellow-green from my pear thread to warm it up. I do this because I know that there is light from the pear reflecting into the cast shadow, causing the pear to influence its tone.

Painting

5. Start by roughing in the very darkest spots, which are the stem and the thin line of the occlusion shadow, with our very dark violet mixture. Then, move on to the next darkest value, which is the core shadow. For this, I use the darkest green on my palette, right below where I added the red.

6. Next, use the next lightest cool tone and block in the reflected light. At this point, it's a good idea to establish some background color and check its relationship with the dark side of the pear. The pear should be a darker value than the background at this point.

7. Working our way clockwise around the pear, paint in the halftones that make up the lit side of the pear. As you do this, you can let your brushstrokes overlap the core shadow just a little bit to soften the edge of the terminator. You will have to wipe your brush often if you do this. Every time you touch the core shadow, your brush will pick up a little bit of the darker color, and if you don't clean it off, you will muddy the yellow-green of the halftone. Continue blocking in background color as you go. The pear should be slightly lighter than the background on the lit side.

8. Now it's time to get the cast shadow and the foreground established. The cast shadow will usually be a little darker nearer to the object and gradually get lighter in value as it moves farther away. Add some foreground color around the base of the pear to check the relationship between pear, cast shadow and foreground.

9. The final stage is to finish covering the background and foreground. I do this first because the white of the panel can throw off how we see the highlights. Once the panel is completely blocked in, I add some light value to the stem—that warm neutral from the cast shadow will do nicely for this. I also reestablish the occlusion shadow if I need to. This should be a subtle accent, so be careful not to overdo it. Now mix just a touch of cadmium yellow lemon with some titanium white to warm it up and add the highlights. I put these on the very lightest part of the halftone. Give it a final look to make sure the shape and color relationships don't need any more adjusting, and you're ready to call it done!

Some Notes on Finishing Paintings

On small studies like the ones in this book, I will adjust and fix obvious errors up to a point. If I just can't get an area to read the way I want it to, I do my best to figure out the issue, but I try not to agonize over it too much. Whatever challenges beleaguered you on one project can easily be addressed when you confront them again in your next painting. Frustration is a poor teacher, and we are better off having another go when we're rested and excited to paint!

PAPER BAG IN WARM AND COOL TONES

Paper bags are wonderful things to paint. The warm, semi-translucent paper creates a perfect opportunity to explore color temperature. The folds and wrinkles of the form, along with its rectilinear disposition, really invite exploration of its planes.

What You'll Need

Panel

Paints: cadmium red light, cadmium yellow lemon, cobalt blue, titanium white

Palette

Palette knife

Brushes

Brush cleaner

Mineral spirits

Paper towels or cloth rags

Ruler

What Do We See?

Our bag is a wonderful combination of warm, neutral planes. The light is coming from the upper right, and the main face of the bag is mostly in shadow. Where the light strikes the bag along its right side and the top flap the tones are warm. It is cooler in the darkest shaded areas, yet there are areas of relative warmth among the shadows where light is reflecting back into the form. The background is my usual raw canvas backdrop, which is also quite warm. I'm going to change that in the painting, though. I feel like a cooler, slightly violet backdrop would be more interesting to surround our mostly warm, neutral bag. I'm also choosing to ignore that line of lettering across the bottom of the bag. I don't think it adds anything to the composition.

STEPHENS
4·20·21

Blocking In Your Subject

1. I'm mixing a little bit of mineral spirits with a bit of cadmium red light this time and starting with a vertical mark to hang my bag on. This vertical line also helps me accurately judge my angles. Once I mark the overall height and width, I block in the big shapes. You will notice that the drawing isn't perfectly faithful to my reference. I wanted the bag to have a little more upright posture, and as long as there are no internal contradictions within the drawing, we will be in good shape!

Mixing Your Colors

2. I start by mixing a vibrant orange with my cadmium red light and cadmium yellow lemon. This will be the base for all of my bag colors.

3. I then add a little bit of cobalt blue to half of my orange. I don't want to add so much that the mixture starts to look blue—I just need enough to make it a little darker and relatively cool when compared to the pure orange.

4. Next, I create two strings of color by gradually adding titanium white to the two sides. I only need a couple of values on the cool side since these will be used on the shaded areas. On the warm side, I will need more of a value range. I want some relatively warm, dark tones for the reflected light in the shaded side as well as some warm, light tones for the lit areas.

5. Finally, I mix my background and cast shadow colors. I start by mixing a dark violet with the cobalt blue and cadmium red light. I then tint that like crazy with titanium white—be sure to save a little bit of the dark violet because we'll need some for the cast shadow. We want the background tone to be just a step darker than the lightest paper bag color. Now mix a lighter version of that color by adding more titanium white and just a touch of cadmium yellow lemon to it. This will be the foreground color. The final element that we need to mix is the cast shadow family. I start with the dark violet and add titanium white until it's the right value. Next, I warm it up with a little bit of our pure orange because I know the side of the bag is reflecting some warm light back into the cast shadow. I never mix just one tone for my cast shadows. Try to keep some variation in your mixture so you have more than one option to test and because we know that cast shadows are rarely only one tone!

Painting

6. I start by roughing in the darkest cool shadows. I use the darkest cool brown just to the left of the mixed orange on my palette.

7. I continue with the warmer sections of the shaded side and I start establishing some of the light halftones on the lit side of the bag. I'm working on these simultaneously so I can check the value relationships.

8

9

8. I work back and forth between lights and darks until the bag is completely blocked in. I'm using my best judgment to differentiate between the warm and cool passages as well as the light and dark values. Use your model as your guide or reference the photo in this book if you're working from that. Remember, we're looking for relative differences in tone. These can be tricky to see, but take heart! As with all things, it becomes easier with practice!

9. Once the bag is blocked in and the internal relationships have been established, I put in the background, foreground and cast shadow.

10. Finally, I finish painting in the background and foreground. At this point, I often use a palette knife to spread the paint on and to straighten and sharpen edges where necessary. I also like using a palette knife here to smooth out any distracting brush textures. This is purely a matter of personal preference. As you continue to paint and look at paintings, you will start to develop your own mark-making vocabulary.

Some Ideas About Using Different Tools

Some painters use a palette knife exclusively to apply paint. Some painters use just brushes. I heard once from a painter friend of mine that someone had said, "If you're going to use a knife, that's all you should use and that if you're going to use brushes, you should limit yourself to just brushes." This is patently ridiculous. I use both all the time as well as rags, fingers, brush handles and whatever else seems like it will get the job done. The painting cops have yet to cite me for these violations. Over time, you will start to gravitate toward whatever tools most easily make the kinds of marks you like to make. This is as it should be, and don't ever let anyone tell you you're doing something wrong!

TACKLING TEXTURES

Every item you will ever paint has its own unique texture. Understanding and recreating the visual clues that describe those textures is endlessly fascinating. Light reacts differently when it strikes different types of surfaces. Generally speaking, the shinier the surface, the more abrupt the transitions between tones. Surfaces that are more textured or less shiny tend to have softer transitions. Learning to carefully observe what we are seeing will help us describe these textures with paint.

STEPHENS
6·27·21

SMOOTH AND SHINY PLUM

Plums make wonderful subjects for painting. The reflections that get picked up by their glossy skins are endlessly fascinating. They also offer a great opportunity to work in a narrow, low-key value range.

What You'll Need

Panel

Paints: cobalt blue, alizarin crimson, titanium white, cadmium red light, cadmium yellow lemon

Palette

Palette knife

Brushes

Brush cleaner

Mineral spirits

Paper towels or cloth rags

Ruler

What Do We See?

Our subject is a slightly irregular dark violet ball. If we look a little closer, we can clearly see the occlusion shadow at the bottom and the core shadow working its way across the middle. The reflected light is a slightly cooler band of color running between these two elements. There are hints of warmer violet in some of the transitions on the lit side of the plum. I've decided to paint this from a vantage point that is a little higher than I would normally choose. It's such a simple object that I want to be sure to include the recess where the stem would be. The concave section adds some interest to an otherwise very simple form.

Mixing Your Colors

2. I start by mixing a dark violet with my alizarin crimson and cobalt blue. I then use titanium white to make a couple of lighter values. Moving back to the top of the left color thread, I then add more alizarin crimson to the dark violet. I repeat my previous steps and make two lighter versions of this red-violet. These six colors will be enough for me to start the plum. I will probably have to adjust them to be lighter as I get closer to finishing, but I want to be careful to not add too much white. One of the things that make plums so interesting to paint is their dark, narrow value range.

Blocking In Your Subject

1. Since the plum is made up of a mostly dark violet tone, I've decided to use cobalt blue mixed with a little bit of of mineral spirits for the initial blocking. I find the vertical center of my panel and map out the basic shapes. On glossier objects like this, the reflection of the cast shadow is on the bottom right of the plum.

3

3. Next, I mix my background and cast shadow colors. I mix a bright orange using cadmium red light and cadmium yellow lemon and add titanium white to it until it's close to the same value as my backdrop. The vibrant orange gets substantially less vibrant as I add titanium white to it. Once I get to the correct value, I can add just a touch of cobalt blue to neutralize it further. To achieve my lighter foreground color, I add more titanium white and just a sliver of cadmium yellow lemon to warm it up. For the cast shadow, I start with orange again and add titanium white until I've approximated the value of the middle of the cast shadow. This is pretty vibrant, so I add a little violet to it. This darkens and cools my tone. I make sure to keep some of the original color intact since there's more than one color in the cast shadow.

4

Painting

4. I establish the darkest darks first with the darkest violet that I mixed. These are located along the bottom of the plum at the occlusion shadow as well as where the cast shadow is reflected in the skin of the plum just above. I also block in the core shadows across the body of the plum and inside the stem hollow.

5. I establish the band of reflected light between the core shadow and the reflection of the cast shadow. This gets a little redder toward the right.

6. I block in the halftones of the lit side of the plum. I'm trying to be sensitive to the temperature shifts as I go. At this point, I start to rough in some background so I can see the color relationships.

7. I then add the cast shadow and the foreground color.

8. In the final phase, I eliminate the white of my panel by continuing the background colors to the edge. Once this is done, I can adjust any edges around or within the plum and add the highlights. These highlights are very light versions of the color I already have here, not pure white, so I just mix a small amount of that with my titanium white. I also soften the transition between the backdrop color and the foreground. The softer this is, the less attention it draws.

Some Notes on Background Colors

When I was teaching high school, my students would very often ask for my advice as to what color they should use for their backgrounds. The short answer was always "whatever you want!" Needless to say, this was seldom very satisfying to them. The point of a background is to make our subject visible. If the background were identical to the subject, the subject would be invisible. We've got to have some contrast or we won't be able to see anything. If you recall the four properties of color—hue, temperature, vibrancy and value—at least one of these things needs to contrast with the focal point of the painting.

In the case of our plum, I've chosen to contrast all four. My plum is a dark value and the background is light. Orange and violet are distinctly different hues, and violet is relatively cool compared to orange. My violets are much more vibrant than the muted orange neutral that I've chosen. It's not necessary to contrast every property of color. Sometimes, one or two works just fine. It's all just a matter of what you want the background to do.

STEPHENS
6·24·21

FUZZY PEACH

Peaches make fascinating and varied subjects. Even a single variety like the yellow peach has a tremendous amount of variation in color ranging from deep red to pale yellow. The fuzzy texture and vibrant colors offer a unique challenge to the still life painter. In this project, we will be softening the edges around and inside of the peach to help describe the fuzzy texture. Skip to the notes at the end of this project for more insight into edges!

What You'll Need

- Panel
- Paints: cadmium red light, cobalt blue, alizarin crimson, cadmium yellow lemon, titanium white
- Palette
- Palette knife
- Brushes
- Brush cleaner
- Mineral spirits
- Paper towels or cloth rags
- Ruler

What Do We See?

This is a fairly typical yellow peach. The local color ranges from pale, vibrant yellow to deep red-violet. There are two areas of core shadow. The main one moves across the body of the peach along the terminator, and the secondary core shadow is on the left side of the concave recess where the stem would go. One of the challenging things about painting peaches is that they often have a range of local colors. We will essentially have to come up with light, medium and dark versions of all the yellow, orange and red hues that make up our subject.

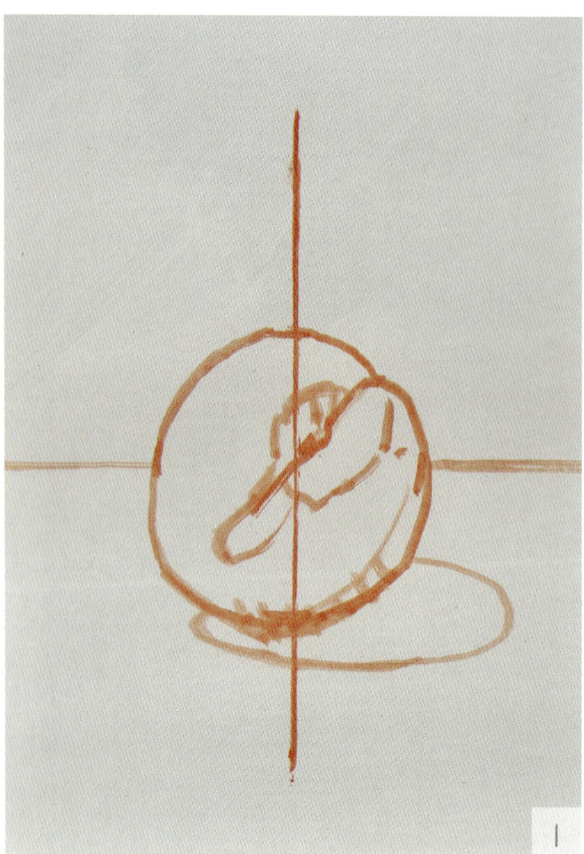

Blocking In Your Subject

1. I'm using cadmium red light and a bit of mineral spirits to get started. As usual, I start with a vertical line to orient the peach and then I add a few marks to place it on my panel. Our subject is essentially a slightly irregular ball. It's roughly as wide as it is tall. One of the interesting things about this subject is the recessed area where the stem goes, so I take a little extra time to map out the structure of this area. Finally, I add the ellipse of the cast shadow at the bottom of the form and the border where my backdrop meets my stage.

Mixing Your Colors

2. I start by mixing a very dark violet with cobalt blue and alizarin crimson. As I move down the thread, I add more alizarin crimson to create a red-violet hue and then I add some cadmium red light to this. Finally, I add a little cadmium yellow lemon at the bottom. Notice that we are moving from a dark and relatively cool color to a lighter and warmer hue.

3. My second thread starts with cadmium yellow lemon mixed with a tiny bit of the violet that I mixed earlier. This will become the areas of yellow that are located in the shaded parts of the peach. As this thread moves down, I transition to pure cadmium yellow lemon, then add a little cadmium red light, making a yellow-orange and an orange, respectively. At this point, you can add a touch of titanium white to the orange—just enough to lighten the value a step but not enough to wash out the vibrancy.

4. The final thread that I will need is the background and cast shadow colors. I start by mixing another batch of violet, but this time, I use cadmium red light and cobalt blue. This will make a less vibrant version of violet than I achieved when I used the alizarin crimson earlier. I then add titanium white to it until I match the value of my background. This grayed-out violet should work well with the yellow and yellow-orange hues of our subject. The foreground is a lighter version of this with just a bit of cadmium yellow lemon added for warmth. For the cast shadow, I add titanium white to the original violet mixture to match the value and then I warm it up with a little orange that I mixed for the peach. This should give me the basic building blocks that I will need for this study. Some cross-mixing between threads may be necessary. Once we start to get a sense of our relationships as we begin to paint, we will have a better idea. We'll cross that bridge when we get to it, though!

Painting

5. I start by roughing in the darkest areas. I use my darkest mixed violet for the occlusion shadow and the stem recess. For the core shadow on the body of the peach, I use the red-violet that is just a little lighter in value. Pay attention to where the local color changes the core shadow. I also paint some of the reflected light using the same dark red-violet. The secondary core shadow at the top of the peach where the stem would reside is mostly the dark neutral yellow we mixed.

6

7

8

6. Next, I establish the reflected-light areas. In this case, I'm using red-orange from my first color thread in the main area and a lighter version of the yellow ochre in the stem recess area.

7. Using the colors from the middle thread, I block in the halftones on the lit side and establish some background color to make sure my relationships are sound.

8. Moving to the bottom of the peach, I then put in the cast shadow. I take the cast shadow color we mixed earlier and then pick up just a bit of the orange and yellow from our middle thread to achieve those reflections from the peach back onto the cast shadow. Next, I surround it with my foreground color to check the relationships.

9. I finish filling in the background and foreground until the whole panel is covered.

10. Once everything is covered, I add some intermediate colors to smooth the transitions where needed and soften the perimeter's edge. I also use my knife to soften the horizontal edge in the background.

Some Ideas Regarding Edges

Edges are very important in painting. If an object is completely surrounded by a hard, sharply delineated edge, it tends to look like a two-dimensional cutout pasted to the painting's surface. Sharp edges do have their place. Areas of greater contrast attract the eye and can be used to lead the viewer around the painting. Soft edges serve to integrate objects into their environment and create opportunities for viewers to participate by allowing them to complete what they see. Edges can be softened in a number of ways. They can be physically blurred by dragging one color into another or by adding an intermediate tone. Some edges can be softened to the point they disappear altogether. You would be surprised how often you can get away with using vanishing edges. I encourage you to experiment and have fun!

STEPHENS
6·28·21

SIMPLIFIED STRAWBERRY

The vibrant reds of strawberries can be incredibly alluring to paint. At the same time, their dimpled texture can be quite intimidating, especially to a painter like me. I tend to be drawn to bigger shapes that I can describe effectively with a few simple brushstrokes. The challenge with strawberries is implying that fussy texture without going crazy. The rich reds combined with successfully implying the texture is very satisfying, so it is worth the challenge!

What You'll Need

Panel

Paints: cadmium red light, alizarin crimson, cobalt blue, cadmium yellow lemon, titanium white

Palette

Palette knife

Brushes

Brush cleaner

Mineral spirits

Paper towels or cloth rags

Ruler

What Do We See?

There it sits, our single strawberry in all its glory. The color ranges from a chromatic black at the bottom through a series of deep reds and red-violets on the shaded side. The reds take on a warmer red-orange tone where the light strikes our subject. The leaves are an appealing assortment of warm greens. Throughout the whole of the strawberry, we see those maddening little seeds that would be so easy to get lost in. I'm going to show you a painless strategy for simplifying all that detail.

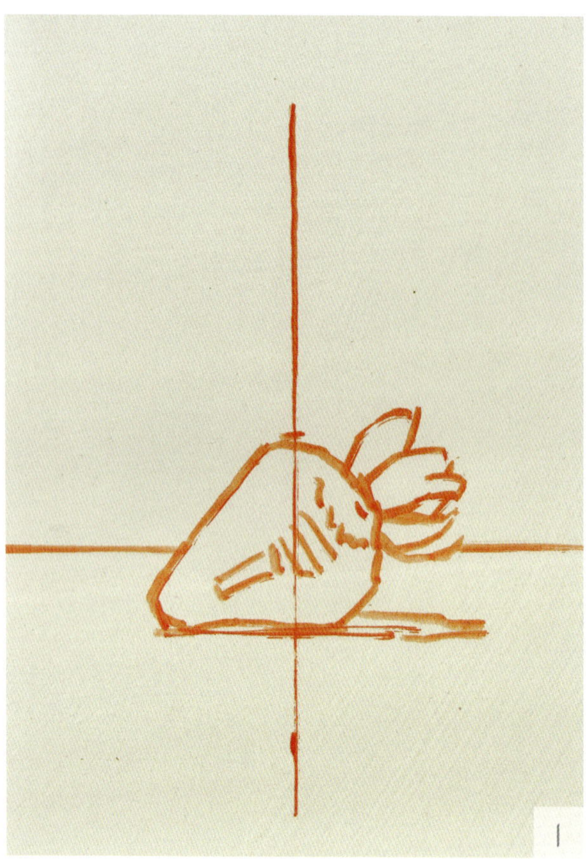

Blocking In Your Subject

1. Cadmium red light mixed with a little bit of mineral spirits seems like the obvious choice for blocking in this subject. After finding the vertical center of my panel, I block in the big shapes. The strawberry is basically a triangle with rounded corners, and the leaves are a series of elongated, irregular football shapes. The cast shadow is narrow on this subject and not terribly long.

Mixing Your Colors

2. I'm going to start by mixing the reds for the star of our vignette. I first mix a dark red-violet with the alizarin crimson and cobalt blue. As I move down the color, I add more alizarin crimson and then some cadmium red light. Continuing down, I add just a touch of cadmium yellow lemon, but not too much! We still want it to look red, just a lighter, warmer version of red. Then I add a small amount of titanium white. These colors will serve for most of the strawberry, but I am going to do some cross-mixing of my threads later.

3. Next come the greens. I'm only going to need three values. I can make slight adjustments to these as needed. I start with a dark green mixed with cobalt blue and cadmium yellow lemon. I then add a small amount of cadmium red light to this. The cadmium red light darkens the mixture and reduces the vibrancy. I then take some of the original green, before I mixed the cadmium red light in, and add a little titanium white. To keep this from looking too chalky, I add a little more cadmium yellow lemon to the mix. The lightest green has a little more titanium white and a touch more cadmium yellow lemon. Notice how the green becomes more of a yellow-green as the value gets lighter.

4. The last color group that I'll need is the background. I think something based on a cool violet will work well with both my reds and my greens. Since I want the background to be fairly neutral, I mix a dark violet with cobalt blue and cadmium red light. The cadmium red light will yield a much less vibrant violet than alizarin crimson would. I add titanium white to approximate the value of my background. For the foreground, I add more titanium white and a sliver of cadmium yellow lemon to warm it up and further neutralize it. For the cast shadow colors, I add titanium white to the dark violet until I get close to the right value and then I add a touch of the red-orange from my strawberry thread to warm it up. Remember, colors from the strawberry are reflecting into the cast shadow. There are not enough to turn the shadow red, but they do warm it up substantially.

5

Painting

5. I start with the darkest hues from my red and green color families. I use the very dark red-violet for the occlusion shadow and a slightly lighter, redder version of that for the core shadow. For the core shadows and dark accents on the leaves, I use my very darkest green mixture.

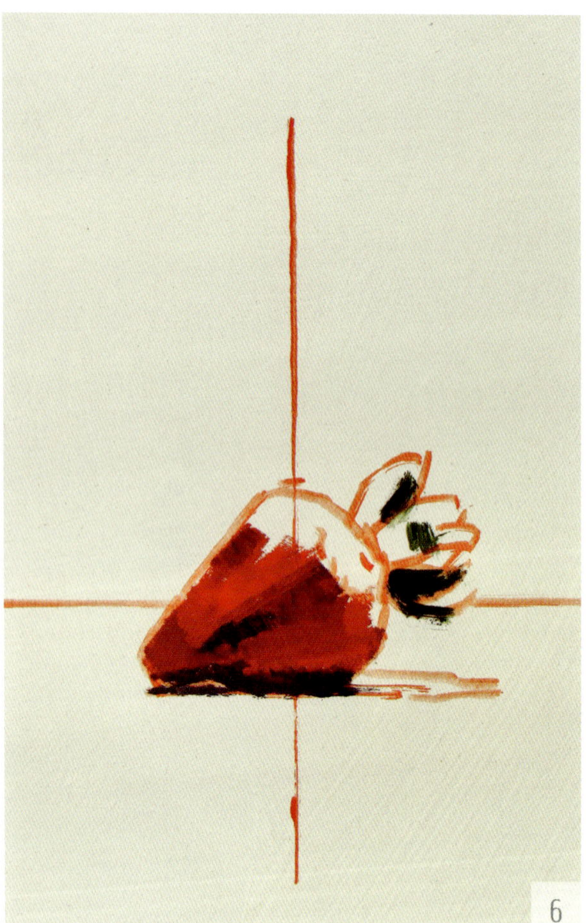
6

7

8

6. I establish the reflected light on the strawberry and start blocking in the vibrant halftones on the lit side. These two values look nearly the same, but it's important to remember that the reflected light will always be a little darker than any area being hit with direct light. I use the value from the middle of my red family for the reflected light and the next lightest color for the lit side.

7. I use my lightest hues from the red color family and establish the lightest value on the strawberry. There is also a very pale green crown around the top of the strawberry where it hasn't quite turned red. I just add a little more titanium white to my lightest green and use that. I overlap the brushstrokes next to the light red to soften that edge as I go. I finish establishing the greens in the leaves using the warm greens that are a step lighter than the strawberry crown. Blocking in some background color helps the whole thing make sense.

8. Next, I add the cast shadow and some foreground color to compare it to.

9. After painting out the rest of the background and foreground, I start addressing that pesky texture. I do this by making a series of marks with my dark violet. I'm using the one made with the cadmium red light that I used as a base for the background. It's a little more opaque than the one made with alizarin crimson. I don't want to be fussy here. I just want to start to indicate some texture. A small, pointy brush works great for this, but you can also use the sharp corner of a flat brush.

10. Once I have the seeds mapped out, I can add some highlights. The dark spots are recessed so I need my highlights to be *around* the recesses. I'm also enhancing the reflected light a little. I mix a little of my dull violet background color with some red-violet strawberry color. I want this to be just a little lighter than the deep red that I already have there. With this mix, I paint around some of the dark dimples in the reflected-light area in the bottom half of the strawberry. The last thing I do is soften the top edge just a little.

Some Notes on "Bad" Paintings

You're going to produce some stinkers in your career. There's no doubt about it. Someone once said that the way to make a good painting is to make a hundred bad ones first. The "hundred" is arbitrary. The point is that you have to make some bad ones initially. Little by little, you will start to figure out how to make things work the way you want them to, and lousy paintings can help you do that. Try not to just write them off as bad. Analyze your failures and try to pin down why they're going to the burn pile. Be as specific as you can and resolve to use that knowledge to improve your next painting. Sometimes, there's more to learn from our failures than from our successes.

JUICY PEACH SLICES

Sometimes, a subject we have already painted can be physically altered in such a way that it becomes completely different. Slicing up a peach does just that. The vibrant yellow-oranges of the fruit are a great counterpoint to the relatively neutral skin, and the repeated shapes of the slices can be a lot of fun to arrange. Additionally, our reference material is now perfectly poised for eating when we're finished with our little study.

What You'll Need

Panel

Paints: cadmium red light, cadmium yellow lemon, cobalt blue, titanium white

Palette

Palette knife

Brushes

Brush cleaner

Mineral spirits

Paper towels or cloth rags

Ruler

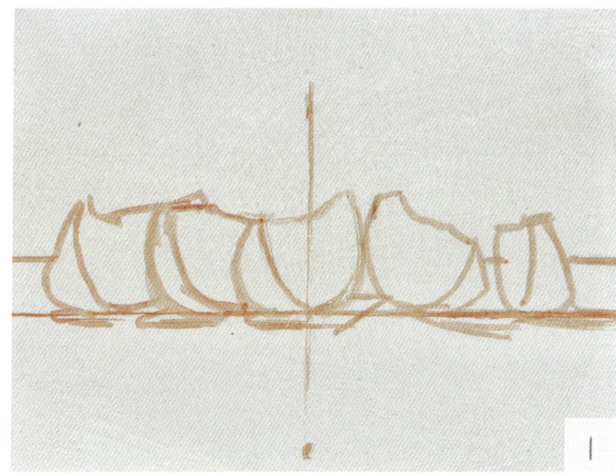

What Do We See?

I've arranged my slices in a row, straight across the stage. The light is coming from the upper left. The visible cut planes of the three slices on the left are in shadow and the two on the right are angled so they are lit. It's a simple arrangement, but I like the repetitive yet varied shapes, and I think the contrast between the vibrant wet planes of the fruit and the slightly dull, dark skin is interesting.

Blocking In Your Subject

1. I start by mixing up some orange with my cadmium red light and cadmium yellow lemon and then I dull it down a little with some cobalt blue. I'm going for a warm tone that isn't too bright. I add a little bit of mineral spirits and find the center of my panel. I then put in a horizontal line where I want my slices to sit. Once I have the horizontal and vertical guides in place, it becomes a matter of visually measuring my reference and transcribing the shapes. This drawing is a bit more complicated than some of the others. I am constantly comparing angles and curves within the drawing to my vertical and horizontal guides. As with all things, this becomes a lot easier with practice.

Mixing Your Colors

2. I start by mixing the dark colors that make up the skins of the peach slices. The local color is already a dark reddish tone, and since the skins all fall in shadow, it is relatively neutral. I start with cadmium red light and add a little cobalt blue to it. I'm not trying to make violet. I want just enough blue to make the red darker. Once I have that, I make a brighter version by adding a little more cadmium red light. I then add some cadmium yellow lemon to warm it up just a bit. I always keep some of the original dark base intact in case I have to make any adjustments later. I then take my new mixture and make a couple of different versions of it, adding more cadmium yellow lemon on the right side and just a touch of titanium white on the left. I want all of these tones to be close to the same value and relatively dark since they are all in the shadows.

3. Next, I mix the colors that will describe the flat planes of the sliced fruit, I start by mixing just a touch of cadmium red light with some cadmium yellow lemon. I don't want to turn my yellow to orange. I'm just making the yellow a little darker and warmer. Moving down, I mix more cadmium yellow lemon with the mixture and then a touch of titanium white to lighten the value. Be careful with the titanium white, though—too much and you will desaturate the yellow!

4. The last color family is the environment. I want something that will make my yellows and yellow-oranges look more vibrant, so I'm going to base my background oil in violet. I use a mixture of cobalt blue and cadmium red light. I then add lots of titanium white to this mixture to match the light value of my background. Because the cadmium red light is so strongly biased toward yellow already, I wind up with a slightly cool, neutral violet tone.

Moving down, I add just a touch of cadmium yellow lemon to this and a bit more titanium white for the foreground color. I then go back up to the original dark violet and add titanium white until I have approximated the value of the cast shadows. I warm this up with some of the amber from my peach skin mixture. The object casting the shadow will usually be influencing the shadow color by reflecting into it.

Painting

5. I start by painting the curved triangle shapes that make up the peach skins. The darker values will be at the bottom at the occlusion shadows. The skins aren't a uniform tone. There is a lot of variation due to the reflected light and natural differences in local color. Try to be sensitive to those subtle shifts in value and temperature. I do this by comparing adjacent tones. If you squint and blur your eyes, it can help simplify what you are seeing. I then block in the shaded sides of the cut planes on the left three slices. I found that I had to mix just a little bit of skin color with my darkest yellow mixture to get this right. I also paint the narrow crescent of cast shadow on the fourth slice from the left.

6

7

6. The next step is to establish the lit areas of the slices on the two rightmost pieces and along the top edge of the other three.

7. Once the peach slices have been blocked in, I put in the cast shadows. These are generally darker near the base of the slices and become more diffused and warmer as they move away. At this point, it's a good idea to get some background color in so that we have something to compare everything to. I want my background to be lighter than the shadowed areas of my subject and darker than the lit areas.

8

8. Before I do my final adjustments, I carry the background and foreground colors all the way to the edges of my panel.

9. Once I have the panel completely covered, I can make whatever final adjustments are needed. Some values need to be lightened to create more contrast with the background, and a few of my transitions need a little softening in the peach skins. I also soften some of the edges in the cast shadows and add that beautiful red accent at the top of the three peaches on the right where the pit was.

Some Notes on Drawing

Drawing is an incredibly important skill when it comes to painting. Sometimes shapes look wrong, but we can't quite figure out what the problem is. In these instances, flipping the piece upside down or looking at its reflection in a mirror can often help us figure out what the issue is. It is always easier to fix a problem with the drawing early, when the paint is thin, rather than later once the layers have built up. As with just about everything in life, the best antidote for poor drawing is regular practice. Anytime you can work from observation in your sketchbook is another brick laid in this important foundation.

KEEPING COLORS BRIGHT AND VIBRANT

Vibrancy is an important element of color that can be tough to get a handle on. You know it's going to be difficult because it goes by so many names. Throughout my years as an art student, and later as a teacher and painter, I've heard it referred to as chroma, saturation and brilliance. Painters sometimes use the word "bright" to describe it. This is, unfortunately, quite close to and often interchangeable with "light," which is a word that describes value.

Vibrancy is, quite simply, the amount of pure hue that a color contains. The most vibrant colors are the colors of the spectrum—red, orange, yellow, green, blue and violet—in their purest form. To the painter, that means straight out of the tube. Anytime we mix anything with one of these hues, we are likely to make it less vibrant. This includes white. If you think about it, it makes sense. When you add white to a hue, there is less of that hue present. It's easy to get chalky, dull colors when lightening the value with just white. Luckily, there are a number of techniques that we can use to work around this sad fact. We are going to explore some of those ideas in this chapter.

STEPHENS
4-15-21

SUMMER FRESH LEMON

Still life painting is the ideal venue for isolating the myriad of visual elements that painters encounter. By selecting a simple lemon for our scrutiny, we are also isolating the color yellow for our consideration. There are more ways to handle yellow than I can count, but this little study will offer some insight and help get us started.

What You'll Need

- Panel
- Paints: cadmium red light, cobalt blue, cadmium yellow lemon, titanium white
- Palette
- Palette knife
- Brushes
- Brush cleaner
- Mineral spirits
- Paper towels or cloth rags
- Ruler

What Do We See?

The first thing we notice about our lovely lemon is the rich yellow color. It has all the elements we've been exploring that help us describe form. There's a dark occlusion shadow, a defined core shadow, reflected light and a nice variety of light and vibrant yellows on the lit side. The cast shadow is elongated and narrow because of the angle of the light source and our eye-level view.

Blocking In Your Subject

1. I'm using cadmium red light mixed with a little bit of mineral spirits to block in the big shapes. I start with a vertical line to center the subject and add a horizontal line to place the bottom of the lemon on and to help align the cast shadow. I then make a few marks to place the lemon on the panel. Next, I rough in the ovoid shape of the lemon and the narrow ellipse of the cast shadow. At this point, you can make a few marks to map out the location and shape of the core shadow.

Mixing Your Colors

2. I start by mixing cobalt blue and cadmium red light to make a dark violet. This will be a useful mixture for adjusting the darker, more neutral yellows of the lemon that are in shadow. I then start with cadmium yellow lemon and add just a touch of my mixed violet to it. It's important that this mixture still reads as yellow, so add just enough violet to make it a darker, duller version of yellow. Once I have a tone that approximates the value of my core shadow, I add more cadmium yellow lemon to make a slightly lighter version. The next step is pure cadmium yellow lemon and the final step has just a touch of titanium white added. We want just enough titanium white to lighten the value and not wash out the vibrancy too much.

3. Next, I adjust my intermediate dark yellow with a small amount of cadmium red light. Again, it's important that this color still be part of the yellow family, so be careful to not add too much cadmium red light! This warmer dark tone will be used for the reflected light.

4. The next step is to mix some background color. We can enhance the vibrancy of our subject by making some informed judgment calls here. The complement of yellow is violet—read more about that on page 20—so it makes sense that the yellow will look more vibrant if we put it on a violet background. I don't want a deep, saturated violet however. That would compete too much with our subject and be too far outside of the range of what we are seeing for the purposes of this study. I'm going to mix a small amount of our mixed violet with titanium white to produce a very light, low key violet. At this point, I can add a touch of cadmium yellow lemon to it to knock the vibrancy out even more. The result is a neutral tone that leans toward violet. I add more titanium white to this mixture plus a touch more cadmium yellow lemon to warm it up and I have our foreground color.

5. The final color family that we will need is for the cast shadow. I start with the mixed violet and add titanium white until it's close to the value of the cast shadow. I then warm it up slightly with some of the burnt yellow-orange that I mixed for the reflected light on the lemon. I'm adding this because I know that light is bouncing off of the lemon into the cast shadow and influencing its tone.

Painting

6. I start with the very darkest value of the occlusion shadow at the bottom of the lemon. So little light gets into that area that it appears almost black. The dark mixed violet will work well for this. Next, I rough in the core shadow and some transitional tones at the bottom.

7. Moving down from the core shadow, I establish the reflected light with the warmer neutral version of yellow that we mixed.

8. Next, I block in the halftones on the light side of the lemon. At this point, it's a good idea to get some background down so we can check the relationships. In this case, I want the shaded part of the lemon to be a darker value than the background and the lit side to be slightly lighter. I also rough in the cast shadow. Remember, the cast shadow will be a little darker and sharper edged the closer it is to the object.

9. Once the cast shadow is in place, we can put in some foreground color to make sure we got the value right

10. Complete the background and foreground. I like to get the whole panel covered before I add any highlights because I don't want the white of my panel competing with them.

11. At this point, I soften the transitions along the terminator and around the reflected light. I also soften the horizontal edge where my backdrop meets the horizontal stage. This helps to de-emphasize that edge and put it more in the background. The last thing I do is add the hotspot or highlight. The texture of lemon skin can create a very complex set of highlights. I'm going to radically simplify this by using a palette knife to apply some white mixed with a tiny amount of cadmium yellow lemon.

Some Notes on Paint Consistency

When you open a new tube of paint, you may notice that the consistency is somewhat variable. One moment, you are happily squeezing some luscious pigment onto your palette and in the next instant a giant blob of linseed oil squirts out. This is a fairly common, if somewhat irritating, occurrence. Continued, vigorous shaking and tube kneading will help. If you've already put it on your palette, you will want to thoroughly mix the oil into the paint. I don't care for paint that is too oily, so I will often scoop it up with a palette knife and put it directly onto a piece of unprimed cardboard. The cardboard acts as a sponge to draw the oil out of the paint, giving it a stiffer consistency.

FRESHLY CUT AVOCADO

Avocados are not very charismatic. They are dark, lumpy things that have very little to recommend themselves to the painter. Cut into one, however, and you have a whole different story. The vibrant greens and yellow-greens combined with the creamy consistency of the avocado flesh are practically begging to be described with oil paint.

What You'll Need

Panel

Paints: cadmium red light, cadmium yellow lemon, cerulean blue, titanium white

Palette

Palette knife

Brushes

Brush cleaner

Mineral spirits

Paper towels or cloth rags

Ruler

What Do We See?

The first thing I noticed is the vibrant color of the flesh. It's greener around the perimeter and becomes paler and yellower as it moves toward the center. The cavity left by the pit is partially in shadow. Notice that there is a streak of slightly darker shadow starting at the bottom and moving upward, dividing the lit crescent of the cavity from the area in shadow. This is the core shadow. The surface area of the core shadow is parallel to the source of the reflected light, and it appears darker and slightly cooler since no light is striking it directly. There is also a very narrow, very dark edge of avocado skin surrounding the perimeter of our shape. It gets a little wider and darker at the bottom left of the avocado. The value of the cast shadow is darkest at the very bottom of the object. In fact, it is so dark that we have trouble distinguishing where the avocado ends and where the shadow begins. At the far-right edge, it makes an abrupt turn back to the right and diagonally upwards as it follows the contours of the canvas draped over the backdrop and stage.

STEPHENS
8 • 6 • 21

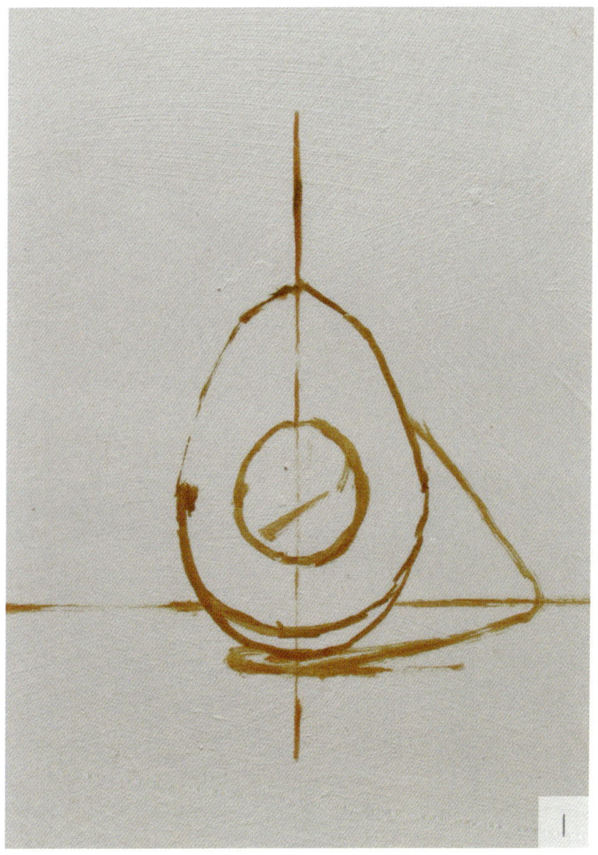

Blocking In Your Subject

1. I start by adding a little bit of mineral spirits to some cadmium red light and cadmium yellow lemon. This will make a vibrant orange, which I will then desaturate with a little bit of cerulean blue. The end result is a desaturated, burnt orange. I'm going to use this to block in the big shapes. I chose this color because I like using a warm neutral for this job. I could just as easily have used some thinned-down cerulean blue. It probably doesn't matter much as it will almost certainly all be covered in the final painting. I'm adding just enough mineral spirits to it so that it flows off the brush like ink. I start with a vertical axis to hang my main shape on and a few small marks to determine its height and width. Once I have an idea of the placement, I simply draw in the large, simplified shapes.

Mixing Your Colors

2. I start by mixing the darker green around the perimeter. It's a straight mixture of cadmium yellow lemon and cerulean blue. Moving down, I combine more cadmium yellow lemon with my mixture and then just a little bit of titanium white.

3. The next color family I'm going to tackle is the avocado flesh inside the shadowed part of the pit cavity. I know that the avocado here is the same local color as it is in the lit area, but it has a darker value and is less saturated than what we can see where the light is striking it. I'm going to start with some of the yellow-green from the middle of my last color thread, just before where I started adding titanium white. I'm going to gradually add just a touch of cadmium red light to this mixture to warm it up and make it a little darker. I need a slightly cooler and darker version for the core shadow as well as a warmer and lighter version to describe the reflected light that is bouncing into that shadow.

4. The final part of the avocado is that very dark, desaturated skin. I'm going to start with my darkest green and add a little more cerulean blue to it so that it's more of a true green than a yellow-green. Adding blue will also make the value a bit darker. Next, I gradually add a small amount of cadmium red light to darken and desaturate the green. Be careful with the cadmium red light—it's a potent pigment and can easily take over a hue!

5

6

7

5. All we have left to mix now are the background colors. I'm going to base my background color on red-violet since it's the complement of yellow-green—read more on that on page 20. I start by mixing my red-violet with cerulean blue and cadmium red light. I then add titanium white until I've matched my background value. I then add more titanium white and a touch of cadmium yellow lemon for the foreground tone. For the cast shadow, I add some titanium white to the original violet mixture until I've approximated the cast shadow value. I also add some cerulean blue to it to cool it down a little.

Painting

6. I'm going to start with the darkest bits first. This is a practical consideration since I'm working on a white panel—the darker colors are going to show up better and I will be able to see what's going on.

7. Next, I indicate the darkest parts of the cast shadow and rough in the darker green around the perimeter of the avocado.

8. I then move on to the core shadow and reflected light in the shaded part of the pit cavity.

9. I need something to compare these shadow colors to, so I add the lit part of the pit cavity. That looks pretty good to me, so I'm going to go ahead and block in the rest of the lit surface of the avocado.

10. Next, I establish my background and foreground colors. I bring these all the way out to the edges of my panel so I can check my other color relationships without them being thrown off by the white of my panel.

11. Once I have the entire panel covered, I can add the highlights. These are pretty close to pure white, but I have added just a touch of cadmium yellow lemon to them to warm them up. I also check and adjust any edges, colors or shapes that may need it.

Some Notes on Varnishing

Varnishing oil paintings can be a hot-button topic among some painters. There are some who never do it and prefer the look of the naked paint. I've even heard some painters go so far as to claim varnishing is somehow dishonest because it hides or alters how the bare paint looks. I have a bit more moderate attitude. You will find that some colors tend to dry with a glossier finish than others. This is usually a function of how much oil is present in the paint or how transparent the color is.

I like the even sheen that my paintings have right when I finish painting them. They have a consistent finish, and the wet sheen is deliciously glossy. Varnishing a painting with a gloss varnish will have the effect of restoring this look. Colors that dried with a matte finish will be restored to their former glory, and the overall sheen of the painting will be restored. Drying time varies radically depending on the weather, brand of paint and any additives that have been used. Very thick passages of paint will dry on the surface, first creating a "skin" over the wet paint underneath. These thick passages can take months to dry completely. As you become more familiar with your materials, you will start to get a good idea of when a painting is dry enough to varnish. At the very least, your painting should be dry to the touch. Varnishing a painting that isn't completely dry will create a mess that can be very difficult to reverse!

STEPHENS
8·1·21

RUBY-RED APPLE

Red delicious apples make great subjects. Their bright red color can be a delightful challenge for the painter. They aren't too round, and their semi-planar quality seems almost custom-made for painting.

What You'll Need

Panel

Paints: cadmium red light, alizarin crimson, cobalt blue, cadmium yellow lemon, titanium white

Palette

Palette knife

Brushes

Brush cleaner

Mineral spirits

Paper towels or cloth rags

Ruler

What Do We See?

The light source is from the upper left, which creates a strong cast shadow on the lower right and a very distinct highlight along the top plane of the apple. The value range goes from a deep red-violet/chromatic black to a very intense, vibrant red on the lit side. There is also a nice variety of more muted light tones in the hollow where the stem is located. The inwardly angled planes of the bottom half catch a great variety of reflected light tones.

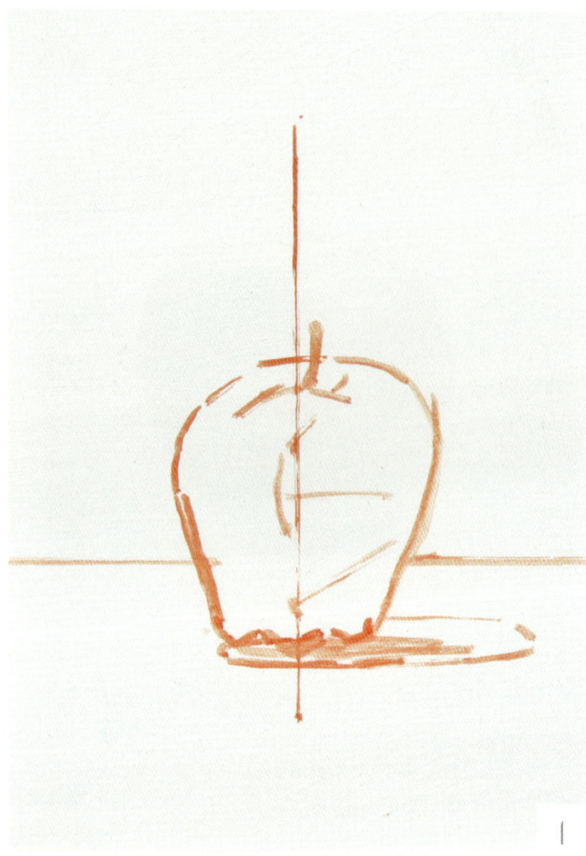

Blocking In Your Subject

1. I use cadmium red light with a bit of mineral spirits to block this one in. I start by finding the center of my panel and drawing a vertical axis to hang my form on. The silhouette is wider at the rounded top, and the sides taper toward the bottom. The cast shadow is a narrow irregular ellipse at the bottom right. I also make a few marks to indicate where the reflections and core shadow are.

Mixing Your Colors

2. I start with alizarin crimson and a little cobalt blue to mix a very dark red-violet. Moving down, I add more alizarin crimson and the cadmium red light. Finally, I add a little bit of cadmium yellow lemon and just a touch of titanium white. This color group will be for the core shadow, reflected light and vibrant directly lit parts.

3. Next, I take the three top dark red-violets and add titanium white. These new tones will be for some of the less saturated light tones at the top of the apple as well as the rim of more violet reflected light on the right side.

4. The final color group that I need to mix contains the background, foreground and cast shadow. I'm going to use a green-based neutral. This will set up a complementary contrast that will make the reds look very vibrant. I mix a medium green with cobalt blue and cadmium yellow lemon. I then add titanium white to it until I match the value of the background. I add cadmium red light to this mixture to dull it down and make it a little warmer, but not too much because I want it to maintain its green character. For the foreground, I add more titanium white to this mixture and a small amount of cadmium yellow lemon. Going back up to my original green mixture, I add titanium white until I match the average value of the cast shadow. I then add some vibrant mixed red from the middle region of my first color group. This tones my mixture down and makes it a little darker. I make sure I have at least two values and temperatures for my cast shadow.

Painting

5. I start with the very darkest red-violets for the core shadow, occlusion shadow, stem and reflection of the cast shadow.

6. I move on to the vibrant reflected light on the lower plane above the cast shadow reflection and the more violet-reflected light on the right edge. I also indicate some of the more muted light tones on the top of the apple near the stem.

7

8

9

7. I continue to the more vibrant reflected lights on the bottom left of the apple and the vibrant light halftones where the light is striking it higher up. I am careful to observe some of the light red-violet reflections on the lower left side. At this point, I also add some background color so that I can evaluate my color relationships more accurately. Right now, the apple is blocked in but looks kind of patchy.

8. Next, I tackle the cast shadow and roughly paint in some foreground color around it.

9. I continue painting, spreading my background and foreground colors all the way to the edges of my panel.

10. The final part of the process is to address the patchiness that I mentioned earlier. I soften the internal edges until the form starts to hold together. I also soften the outside edge, especially on the upper-right side, so that the form is a little more integrated into its surroundings. For the final step, I add the bright highlights with my knife. Pure white would probably work, but I prefer to add a tiny bit of cadmium yellow lemon to warm it up.

Some Notes on Blending

When I was teaching high school, my students would often ask me about blending. They were mesmerized by smooth gradations going from one color to the next. The mechanics of blending colors is a skill that is fairly easy to learn, especially with oil paint, which takes a long time to dry and stays workable for an extended period. Creating smooth transitions between colors is a useful skill, and you will use it from time to time. However, over the course of doing thousands of little paintings, I have come to the conclusion that my paintings look more spontaneous and lively if I can place two carefully observed colors next to each other and have them function as intended without blending.

The more comfortable you get with painting, the more you will start figuring out the kind of look you are drawn to. I prefer a more painterly look. But many very fine painters choose a more finished, naturalistic style. This apple study is a great example of when more blending made sense to me. There were so many tonal shifts that it looked very patchy to me until the very end when I softened—synonymous with blended—all of those internal edges.

TANTALIZING TRANSPARENCY

Painting transparent objects is always an interesting challenge. It seems so counterintuitive to paint something that has no color. I'm sure my high school students got tired of my usual jokey comment that you just have to use clear paint! Obviously, using clear paint is a silly solution, but it kind of illustrates what the challenge entails.

When we look at a clear glass bottle, we are seeing right through it, but the glass is doing a couple of things that allow us to differentiate it from the background. The next few exercises will help us figure out some simple strategies for approaching this challenging and fascinating topic.

STEPHENS
6·28·21

CRYSTAL CLEAR BOTTLE

Let's start with just an empty, clear glass bottle to isolate the elements that we will be looking at when we try to describe transparency with paint. The subtle distortions and reflections created by these simple glass forms can be enrapturing.

What You'll Need

Panel

Paints: cobalt blue, cadmium red light, cadmium yellow lemon, titanium white

Palette

Palette knife

Brushes

Brush cleaner

Mineral spirits

Paper towels or cloth rags

Ruler

What Do We See?

Two things are going on when we look at a clear glass bottle. The glass is transparent, so we can see right through it, but it distorts light as the thickness of the glass changes. This is one reason why we can see an edge around a good portion of the bottle's perimeter. The glass is also reflective. The reflections allow us to get a sense of the surface of the bottle. You will notice that I have set the bottle up on my stage at eye level. This vantage point shows me a very descriptive silhouette while it eliminates some tricky perspective issues. This way, we can concentrate on describing the glass without getting bogged down in the drawing.

Blocking In Your Subject

1. I'm going to use a burnt orange mixed from all three primaries to block this in. Any color will do, but since this piece is made up of subtle neutral tones, I feel like it's a good idea to use one for my layout. I start with a vertical mark in the center and then I hang a rectangle on that. This will be the body of our bottle. Once I have the main mass of that big shape established, I can modify it by rounding the corners and drawing in the neck and shoulders. As always, I am moving from big simple shapes to smaller, more complex ones. Where the glass curves around, there are going to be some subtle tonal shifts in the interior of the bottle. I make sure to indicate where these are as well.

Mixing Your Colors

2. For this painting, I am going to use a set of three secondary colors. Each one is going to be neutralized slightly by its complement. I start by mixing a violet with cobalt blue and cadmium red light. I then lighten the value with titanium white until it's equal to about a 50 percent gray. From that point, I add more titanium white and create a color string that ends just short of white. Next, I mix green with the cobalt blue and cadmium yellow lemon. I then add titanium white until I've matched the color range of my violet thread. The final color I mix is orange using cadmium red light and cadmium yellow lemon. This will be the most vibrant secondary color, so I add a small amount of cobalt blue to dull it down. I then add titanium white to match the values of the two previous mixtures. Notice that as the color families get lighter, their differences become more subtle. I will be doing a fair amount of cross-mixing between these groups.

3

4

Painting

3. I start by establishing the darkest parts of the bottle. A "high key" painting is a painting that is predominantly light in value. This bottle is a good example of that, so the darks are only going to be as dark as the medium-toned values we mixed earlier. I'm trying to be sensitive to subtle temperature shifts here. Most of the darks are cool neutral greens and violets on the top, bottom and edges of the bottle, as well as a slightly lighter violet tone on the upper, left and front-facing planes. I also take this opportunity to establish the cast shadow.

4. Since the bottle is transparent, most of the colors used to paint it will be some variation of the background color. I'm going to use the warm, orange-based neutral. I'm using a bit of the background color in the neck of the bottle and some foreground color at the bottom where it's showing through the glass. I want to get some of the background established early so I have something to compare all the other colors to.

5. I continue with the warm background tones inside the perimeter of the bottle. I'm looking for areas that are either lighter or darker, warmer or cooler, than the base background color. A couple of examples of this are the light reflections along both sides of the bottle and the slightly darker warm tones in the front plane.

6. I paint the background all the way to the edges of the panel after getting the bottle completely blocked in. I'm paying attention to the outside edge of the silhouette. Some areas are lighter than the background, some are darker and, in some spots, the edge disappears completely.

7. Once the entire panel is covered, I put in the very lightest highlights using pure white mixed with just a touch of color from the orange color thread. I also reestablish any dark accents that may be needed. In general, the highlights will be located where the glass curves in such a way that it reflects light directly back at the viewer's eye. These areas are most obvious at the neck of the bottle and around the rim. The darkest areas tend to be along the bottom of the bottle where we are seeing the thickness of the glass edge.

Some Notes on Isolating Color

The tonal shifts that you will encounter when describing transparency with paint will often be very subtle and difficult to see initially. One thing that can be a huge help is a color isolator. A color isolator is simply a card with a small hole punched in it. You can hold this up at arm's length and use it to isolate any color in your reference from the colors that surround it. It is surprising how much easier it is to see the value or relative temperature of a color once it has been removed from its context. A color isolator can be particularly helpful where the tonal shifts are very subtle as in this bottle painting.

STEPHENS
7·14·21

WATERY JAR WITH PAINTBRUSH

Sometimes prosaic items from your studio can be fantastic objects for painting. A simple brush in a jar of water can afford us a whole world of possibilities. The distortions created by the glass and water combined with the subtle value shifts can be wonderful places for the painter to frolic.

What You'll Need

- Panel
- Paints: cadmium red light, cadmium yellow lemon, cobalt blue, titanium white
- Palette
- Palette knife
- Brushes
- Brush cleaner
- Mineral spirits
- Paper towels or cloth rags
- Ruler

What Do We See?

The light is striking our setup from the upper left. You will notice that the paintbrush follows the rules that we have thus far become familiar with—that is, it is lit on the left side and dark on the right. The same is true of the jar above the waterline. It is generally lighter on the left side where it is closer to the light source. The observant painter will notice, however, that the jar below the waterline is exactly opposite. The left side, which is facing the light source, is darker than the right side, which is away from our lamp. This is because the water filling the jar creates a lens and causes it to interact with the light source differently than the empty part of the jar. Some other interesting distortions are the threads on the jar that cut through and distort the brush handle as well as the magnification that occurs where the brush enters the water.

Blocking In Your Subject

1. I start by finding the center of my panel so I can place the subject on it. The jar is placed on the stage at eye level so that its silhouette is a long rectangle and the brush extends upward diagonally from the lower-left corner. I'm using a warm neutral mixture consisting of cadmium red light, cadmium yellow lemon, a bit of cobalt blue and a bit of mineral spirits to block in the large shapes of this study.

Mixing Your Colors

2. The bulk of this painting is going to be composed of variations of the background color. I choose a green-based neutral to contrast with the reds in the paintbrush. I begin by mixing up a medium green from the cadmium yellow lemon and cobalt blue. I add titanium white to this mixture until I have something approximating the average value of the background. I then add a small amount of cadmium red light to further neutralize the green. Moving down, I add more titanium white and a small amount of cadmium yellow lemon until I have a couple of lighter and slightly warmer options to choose from. The lightest value here will become the foreground. I also mix a darker and cooler version that has a little more cobalt blue in it. This will serve for some of the darker accents in the glass and parts of the cast shadow.

3. The next color family that I'll be needing is for the paintbrush. I start with cadmium red light and darken it with a little bit of cobalt blue. I'm not trying to turn the mixture violet—I just want it to be a darker, more neutral version of red. Next, I add some cadmium yellow lemon to the pure red and lighten that with titanium white. This will serve for the parts of the brush where the paint has flaked off the handle and the wood is exposed. It's a good idea to have lighter and darker versions of this color to describe the play of light across it.

4. The final color group that we'll need is a cool gray for the metal brush ferrule. I start by mixing a cool violet with the cadmium red light and cobalt blue. I then add some titanium white to it to match the average value. At this point, I add a small amount of cadmium yellow lemon to produce a more neutral gray. Adding a little more titanium white produces a lighter version, and I'm ready to go.

5

Painting

5. I start by establishing the dark edge along the left side of the jar below the waterline. I'm using the darkest neutral greenish tone at the top of the color thread for this. I also rough in the dark accents at the bottom of the jar. At this point, I go ahead and establish the right side of the jar as well. It's not one of the darker elements, but I feel like it's important to start getting some background color down. When painting transparent objects, it can be very helpful to establish these relationships early.

6. I fill out the jar and part of the adjacent background. I also start blocking in some of the dark tones at the bottom of the brush, including the metal ferrule.

7. I continue moving up the brush handle, establishing the lights and darks for the metal ferrule and the wooden brush handle that is in the jar. I'm taking careful note of the distortions caused by the water surface and the undulations of the jar at its mouth.

Some Notes on Master Studies

A master study is basically a copy of another artist's work. The artist being copied need not be an actual "master"—they just need to have done something that you want more insight into. Painters have been making master copies for centuries, and they are fantastic tools for learning. In the past, these paintings were done for the sole benefit of the artist doing them and were rarely, if ever, shared. In our modern age of social media, there is a great temptation to share everything we do. This is fine, but it is incumbent upon the painter to acknowledge and give full credit to the original artist. If the original artist is alive and you are able to contact them, I would say that the most polite thing to do would be to ask them before sharing.

8. I finish off the rest of the brush handle and surround it with my background color. I also put in the cast shadow and surround that with my foreground color.

9. I bring the background and foreground colors all the way out to the edges of my panel. At this point, I can see the color relationships much more clearly, and I can start adjusting them where needed. I also use my knife to straighten some of the edges of the brush and jar. Once these details are taken care of, I add the highlights on the jar threads and rim as well as on the metal brush ferrule. These highlights are on the cool side so I use pure white. I also add the light streak in the cast shadow caused by the lens that the water creates. This is slightly warmer, so I mix a touch of my foreground color with pure white.

STEPHENS
7·13·21

REFRESHING LEMON WATER

Hopefully by now, you've developed a taste for describing the subtleties of transparency with paint. I've always found it to be among the most engaging and challenging subjects. For this project, I'm going to add a vibrant wedge of lemon to a glass of water. This will combine a blast of saturated color with the closely related tones that we're going to use to describe the transparent elements.

What You'll Need

Panel

Paints: cadmium red light, cadmium yellow lemon, titanium white, cobalt blue

Palette

Palette knife

Brushes

Brush cleaner

Mineral spirits

Paper towels or cloth rags

Ruler

What Do We See?

The light is striking our little tableau from the upper left, brilliantly lighting the rind of our lemon wedge. The inside of the lemon is a very neutralized yellow. The glass and water are transparent, so they will be built with variations of our background color. The left side of the glass below the waterline is a darker value than what is behind it, and the right side below the waterline is a little lighter. There are some dark areas at the bottom of the glass, and at the top, above the waterline, additionally, there are areas where the edges vanish entirely.

1

2

3

4

Blocking In Your Subject

1. I start with a vertical center mark to place our subject. I'm using a warm neutral tone, made by adding a touch of cobalt blue to an orange that I mixed with my cadmium red light and cadmium yellow lemon combined with a touch of mineral spirits, to lay this out. The top of the glass is situated at about eye level, making it a straight edge. The bottom of the glass has a slight downward arc because it's a little bit below eye level and the outer edges of the glass taper slightly toward the bottom. The lemon wedge is a modified semicircle peeking just out of the waterline. The cast shadow extends horizontally to the right.

Mixing Your Colors

2. I'm going to mix the vibrant lemon rind colors first. I start by mixing a tiny amount of cadmium red light with my cadmium yellow lemon. I want just enough to warm the yellow up a little. I want to avoid turning it orange by adding too much cadmium red light. Moving down, I combine more cadmium yellow lemon with the mixture and end by adding a touch of titanium white, being careful to not wash out the color.

3. The next color group I'll mix is the pulp of the lemon. This is a very desaturated yellow, so I start by mixing some violet out of cobalt blue and cadmium red light. I'll be using this to tone down the vibrancy of my yellow. Then, I mix some very pale yellow by combining titanium white with the cadmium yellow lemon. I then tone it down a little further by adding a very small amount of my mixed violet. I add a little more titanium white so that I have a light and a slightly darker version of this color. The last thing I need in this group is some cool light tone for the edge of the lemon rind. I make this by mixing a small amount of the mixed violet with titanium white.

4. The last color group that I'll be needing is the background and foreground colors. I'm going to mix a green-based neutral for this. I start with a cool green by combining cobalt blue and cadmium yellow lemon. I'm using the pure hue here, not a yellow from my mixed group. I add titanium white until I match the average value of my backdrop. I then add a very small amount of cadmium red light to this to neutralize it further. I always try to keep a small amount of my previous color iterations when painting glass. Those different values and tones will be useful later. For the foreground, I add more titanium white and a touch of cadmium yellow lemon to warm things up.

Painting

5. I start with the darkest neutral green colors from my background color family along the top rim, left side and bottom of the glass. I also add a very thin stroke down the right side of the glass. Some of this will end up getting covered later.

6. Early on, I want to get some background color inside and around my glass. It's important to start establishing those relationships as early as we can.

7. Next, I establish the yellows in the lemon. The yellows I'm using are basically either light or dark depending on where they fall in relation to the light source. The skin is vibrant and a bit darker at the top where it peeks out of the water. There is also a darker streak in the middle just below the light band where the water surface is reflecting onto it. The very bottom gets a bit lighter still because of the light reflecting up from the stage. The pulp of the lemon is composed of the neutralized yellows we mixed and is darker at the top and lighter toward the bottom. I also block in the lightest colors in the glass and continue establishing the background color around the perimeter. The cast shadow, which I forgot to mix ahead of time—hey, it happens sometimes—is the same dark neutral green that I used on the left side of the glass with just a touch of cadmium red light to warm it up.

8. Once I have my subject completely established, I can finish filling in the rest of my panel out to the edges.

9. In the final stage, I add the yellow reflection at the top of the glass, add the highlights and straighten up my edges with the knife. I also add the bright refracted light that is shining into the base of the cast shadow.

Some Notes on Palette Management

Working on your palette is sometimes an underappreciated aspect of painting. I have found that the more organized that I can be on my palette, the more freely I can apply the paint to my actual painting. I always put my colors on my palette in the same order. I want to be able to find the color I need without having to think about it. I want the major color groups that I mix to be organized and accessible. This is important so that when I start painting, I won't have to pause and interrupt my flow to do any more major mixing. The cast shadow color that I forgot to mix beforehand on this project is a case in point. I had enough versions of my background colors put together that it didn't take too much to warm up a small amount of the appropriate color to use for that shadow.

REFLECTING ON REFLECTIONS

For me, there's almost nothing more fun to paint than a reflective metal surface. The illusion of volume paired with the shiny surface is intoxicating and so satisfying when you pull it off. It can seem almost magical. As a teacher, I have found this to be one of the most intimidating subjects for beginning painters, but it needn't be. We can analyze what we see and put it into the context of what we know about how light and color interact to chart our way to a successful outcome!

STEPHENS
5-2-21

CHROME COFFEE CREAMER

I have a pretty nice collection of small metal creamers and teapots. I find some of them at thrift stores, but a couple were procured from my favorite local diners. Over the years, I have become a lot less self-conscious about asking to borrow or buy such things when I see something that would make an interesting painting. I like the sleek, simple lines, and the reflections are endlessly fascinating to paint.

What You'll Need

Panel

Paints: cobalt blue, cadmium red light, titanium white, cadmium yellow lemon

Palette

Palette knife

Brushes

Brush cleaner

Mineral spirits

Paper towels or cloth rags

Ruler

What Do We See?

Our subject is a simple steel creamer. It's slightly taller than it is wide, and I've placed it on the stage at about eye level. This will allow us to paint the most simplified and descriptive silhouette. I often place my subjects at eye level for this reason. I want to avoid more complex drawing perspectives and focus on creating color relationships that describe the form and surface quality of the object. The planes of the form that face downward are reflecting the light foreground color. Notice that the cast shadow is clearly reflected in the bottom third of the creamer. The dark middle section of the creamer is reflecting my studio wall directly behind me. The light streaks that are just left of center are reflections of my studio windows.

Blocking In Your Subject

1. I start by mixing up some cobalt blue with a little bit of mineral spirits. When choosing a color to do your layouts, the only real consideration is that you choose a color, or mixture of colors, that won't bother you if some of it is still showing in your finished painting. I feel like the blue will work out well with the cool colors in this subject. I start by blocking in a rectangular shape that is roughly the same proportions as the creamer's. I then round the corners and add the spout and handle. I take a little extra time to indicate where the major shapes are in the reflection.

Mixing Your Colors

2. I'm seeing a lot of dark values in our subject. I decide to go with violet, since that is the darkest color I can mix. Using cobalt blue and cadmium red light, I mix two versions of violet. The one on the left is blue-violet and the one on the right is red-violet. I then make a couple of lighter values of each mixture by adding increasing amounts of titanium white to each. I may need to do some adjusting to these colors as I paint, but I think these six colors should work for most of the creamer.

3

4

5

3. The only other color group that I need will be the background and foreground colors. The cast shadow will be a variation of these. I think a pale muted green will be a good counterpoint to the violets in the creamer, so I start by mixing cobalt blue and cadmium yellow lemon to make a medium green. I mix a good amount of titanium white with this until I've approximated the value of the background, and then I add a very small amount of cadmium red light to this mixture to dull it down a little further. This will be my background color. Moving down from there, I add more titanium white to further lighten the value and just a touch of cadmium yellow lemon to warm my mixture up. For the cast shadow, I take some of my original green mixture and add titanium white to match the average value of the cast shadow, and then I add some cadmium red light to it to neutralize the green. I add a little more titanium white and a sliver of cadmium yellow lemon to create a second, lighter version of the cast shadow color.

Painting

4. I start by roughing in the darkest values. These are along the top and middle of the reflection, around the handle and the occlusion shadow at the bottom. I also take the darkest version of my cast shadow color and establish the reflection of the cast shadow.

5. I continue blocking in the lighter darks in the reflection. I'm being sensitive to the temperature shifts as I alternate between the blue-violet and red-violet mixtures. I also add a little bit of dark blue-green from initially mixing the background color to the darkest reflection in the center, as well as some lighter yellow-green for the reflections of my studio windows.

6. I take my lightest blue-violet mixture and establish the outermost sides of the creamer. This is where the creamer turns and is reflecting the relatively light sides of the inside of my stage box. At this point, it is a good idea to get some background color down so we can check the color relationships. I want the violet on the edge of the creamer to be a slightly darker value than the background.

7. Now I paint the reflection of the foreground color, the cast shadow and the foreground color itself. There are some areas where the stage gets lost on the bottom of the creamer. However, there are enough clues for the viewer to complete the form, so I leave it alone. It's not necessary to define every last part of your painting. Lost edges are a great opportunity for your viewer to participate and engage with your study.

8. Once I finish filling in the painting all the way to the edges, I add the highlights. Pure white would do, but we have to remember that titanium white is a cool color. I use the tiniest amount of cadmium yellow lemon to warm my highlight color up. I also take this opportunity to adjust any shapes and edges as needed.

Some Thoughts on Working from Photographs

Photographs can be a great source of reference material, but it's important to understand their limitations. One of the advantages of working from photos is that the work of flattening the image has already been done. The artist doesn't have to transcribe three-dimensional information onto a flat surface, which can simplify the drawing process.

The major disadvantage to working from photos is that a camera cannot do what your eyes can. When you look at a physical object, your eye automatically adjusts to the amount of light it is receiving. When you look at shadows, your eye is getting less light and your pupil dilates, allowing more light in. This makes more detail visible in the shadowed areas and makes them appear lighter. When we look at the lighter areas of a scene, our pupils contract and let less light in, again allowing us to see more because there is less glare.

A camera cannot adjust on the fly like this. It can only record an average of what is in front of it in the instant that the shutter is activated. For this reason, shadows often look too dark and lack detail in photographs since they are most often more sensitive to the lit areas of a scene. Photos can be a fantastic supplement to our reference material as long as our painting is grounded in working from life and we understand where adjustments need to be made. This creamer is a perfect example of how photographs tend to overly darken some shadow information. Hopefully, at some point in your painting career, you will have the opportunity to compare a live setup with a photograph.

STEPHENS
5·27·21

DAZZLING CHRISTMAS ORNAMENT

Glass Christmas ornaments are a fantastic opportunity to explore reflective surfaces. They have the added advantage of being available in lots of colors other than silver. The distorted reflections of a spherical mirror offer the painter a wide range of possibilities.

What You'll Need

- Panel
- Paints: cadmium red light, alizarin crimson, cobalt blue, titanium white, cadmium yellow lemon
- Palette
- Palette knife
- Brushes
- Brush cleaner
- Mineral spirits
- Paper towels or cloth rags
- Ruler

What Do We See?

I've chosen a red ornament and placed it at about eye level. Our ornament is essentially a ball, so its silhouette will be the same regardless of our viewing angle. The cast shadow, however, becomes an elongated ellipse when seen from this vantage. The red color of our subject is absolute and will actually simplify our color strategy somewhat. The top half of the ornament contains the darker and more complicated reflections of my surroundings, while the bottom half is reflecting the stage surface and the cast shadow.

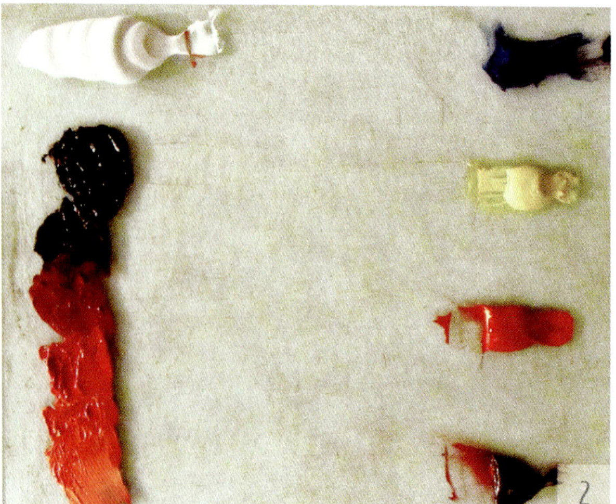

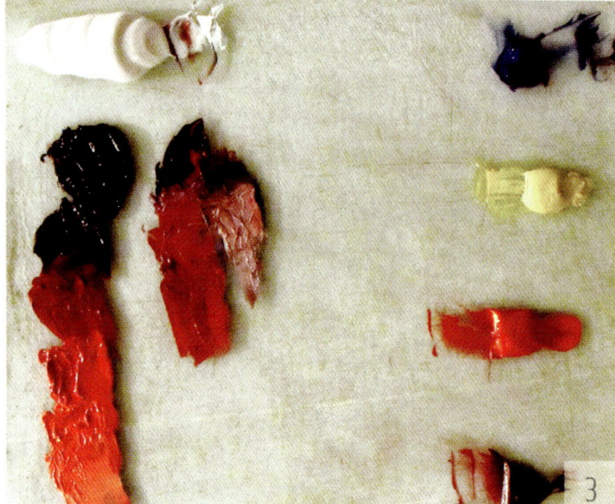

Blocking In Your Subject

1. I start with a vertical and a horizontal axis located in the center of my panel. I'm using a mixture of straight cadmium red light and mineral spirits for this. I make sure the height is equal to the width and sketch in a circle. If the circle isn't perfect, I can adjust it as I go. I just need to get it close for now. I locate and add the hanger at the bottom right of my ball and loosely sketch in some of the details in the reflection.

Mixing Your Colors

2. I start with a mixture of alizarin crimson and cobalt blue. I want a red-violet that will double as chromatic black. Moving down from this, I add more alizarin crimson and then introduce cadmium red light. Continuing down, I add more cadmium red light and then a little bit of titanium white and some cadmium yellow lemon to help maintain the vibrancy.

3. Next, I grab some red-violet from our previous color group and add some cadmium red light to it. To this mixture, I add some titanium white. This will be for the slightly less vibrant areas of red located primarily around the perimeter of the globe.

4. For the background, I'm going to use a neutralized green. I start by mixing a medium green with cobalt blue and cadmium yellow lemon. I then add titanium white until I match the value of the background. I add a sliver of cadmium red light to this to remove some of the vibrancy. Moving down, I add more titanium white and a little bit of cadmium yellow lemon for the foreground. For the cast shadow, I take some of my original green mixture and add titanium white until I've matched the average value of the cast shadow. I then add cadmium red light to this mixture to warm it up. This will also darken the value, so I will have to add more titanium white to a portion of this to get a lighter version of the cast shadow color.

5

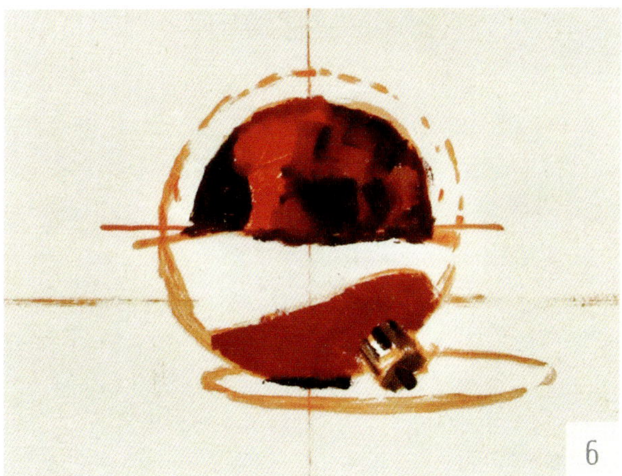

6

Painting

5. I start with the darkest areas of the reflection in the top half of the ornament. I also add the occlusion shadow at the bottom.

6. Next, I establish the middle-range dark reds in the top half and the reflection of the cast shadow. The reflection of the cast shadow looks a little light at this point, but it will start to read as a shadow once I establish the lighter reflection of the stage in the next step. I then paint the dark areas on the hanger, and I use some of the grayed-out tones of the cast shadow colors to establish the silver grays.

7. I add the vibrant light red to the bottom of the ornament and some of the more neutral light reds to the sides of the ball's perimeter. I also add the relatively warm cast shadow. I'm careful to observe where the cast shadow changes value, especially closer to the ornament.

8. I complete the top of the perimeter of the ornament and block in the entire background and foreground. This is a good time to check all of the value relationships, especially the cast shadow.

9

9. At this point, I adjust any shapes that need it and soften some edges around the perimeter of the globe. I also add the highlights. I use titanium white with a very small amount of cadmium red light added. On the primary highlight at the top left of the ornament, I add a small speck of pure titanium white to the center.

Some Notes on Difficulty

Some subjects will seem harder or more difficult than others. When I was teaching high school kids, I would often hear them talking about the relative difficulty of their subject matter choices. It got me thinking about difficulty in painting. It seems to me that the basic tasks of mixing colors and applying paint are constants in the painting process. You might be applying paint to smaller areas that have less tolerance for inaccuracy or trying to create color combinations that are more complex than others, but the relative difficulty of any given task is always going to be about the same.

I know that sometimes I am challenged by drawing an unfamiliar perspective or object, but I try to not quantify it as "difficult." Instead, I try to figure out the specific challenges and then take steps to meet them. The point is that some things are unfamiliar and might be more complicated than what you are used to, but if you brand them intrinsically "hard," it could discourage you from taking a stab at them. I think a much better strategy is to think of everything as doable—things seem a lot less daunting if you can figure out what the challenges are and then take steps to meet them.

TEA(POT) TIME

I first ran across one of these small teapots at a local diner and I was struck by what an interesting subject it would make for painting. I told my waitress what I had in mind and asked where the restaurant got its teapots. She laughed and told me I could just take it. I did and left her a big tip. Over the years, I have found several more at thrift shops and garage sales. I've found that the more I paint, the more I look at the world with an eye toward painting. You never know when something worthy of describing with paint will cross your path.

What You'll Need

Panel

Paints: cadmium red light, cobalt blue, titanium white, cadmium yellow lemon

Palette

Palette knife

Brushes

Brush cleaner

Mineral spirits

Paper towels or cloth rags

Ruler

What Do We See?

Our teapot is a bit more complex than the creamer or the Christmas ornament. It is important to remember that it follows the same rules as our other objects. The downward-facing planes on the pot, handle and spout reflect the surface that the teapot is sitting on. The planes facing us, that are more or less parallel to the direction of both the direct light and reflected light, are the darkest values. Finally, the top planes that are being struck by our light source most directly are very light in value and contain most of the highlights.

Blocking In Your Subject

1. I use cadmium red light mixed with a little bit of mineral spirits for this layout. The body of the teapot below the lid is about as wide as it is tall, so I start by finding the center of my panel and drawing a square. I then add a slight downward arc at the bottom, round the lower corners and taper the sides toward the top. Once the body has been established, I add the lid, handle and spout. I use my vertical centerline to compare angles to and I check to make sure my relative sizes are correct. When drawing relatively complex forms, I always try to break them down into their component parts and to simplify them as much as possible, working from large to small shapes.

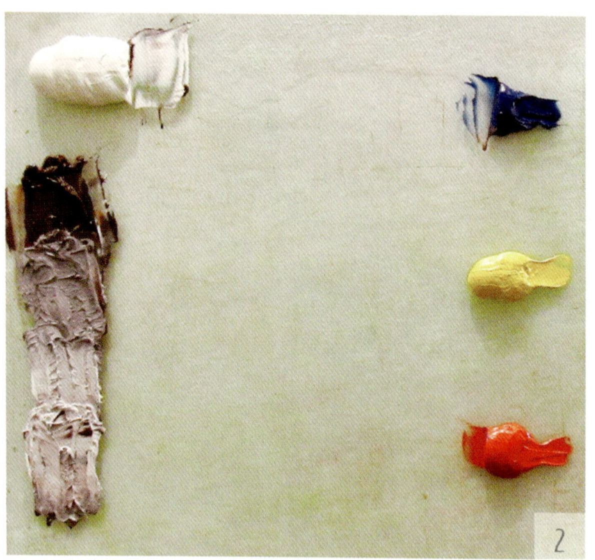

Mixing Your Colors

2. I start by mixing my darkest values. The cool, metallic grays have a little bit of a violet cast to my eye, so I start with cadmium red light and cobalt blue to mix a very dark violet. I then add titanium white to this as I move down the palette until I have four or five values ranging from dark, chromatic black to a medium gray-violet.

3. I'm only going to use two color families for this painting, so the next batch I mix is going to be based on green. I start with a dark blue-green that is composed of cobalt blue and cadmium yellow lemon. I then add a small amount of titanium white to it until I match the value of my second violet value. I will use these two dark blue-green values to help describe the dark tones of my teapot. I then add more titanium white to my second mixture until I have approximated the background value of my setup. This is looking a bit too green to me, so I neutralize it with a thin slice of cadmium red light. I'm careful to not add too much because I want to maintain its green character. I then add more titanium white to this mixture and a little bit of cadmium yellow lemon to brighten the mixture for the foreground. These background and foreground tones will figure heavily in our subject as reflections. For the cast shadow, I move back up to my dark green and add titanium white to match the average value of my cast shadow, and then I warm it up with some cadmium red light. I add some titanium white to part of this so that I have more than one version.

Painting

4. I start with the very darkest parts. These will be the occlusion shadow at the bottom and the darkest, mostly front-facing reflections in the body, handle and spout. They also occur along the front-facing edge of the lid. I use the darkest violet mixture for this.

5

5. I then move on to the secondary darks. For these, I use a combination of the next value step in both my violet and mixed green in some areas. I'm seeing a little more green tones to the right of the teapot. If you are having trouble seeing these subtle shifts in hue, don't worry. I sometimes think I just imagine them! The important thing is to get the value dialed in. Remember, if we can be accurate with our values, the hue will look right! I also use the darkest cast shadow color to establish the reflection of the cast shadow at the bottom of the teapot.

6. I'm now ready to lay in the medium violet tones along the edges of the teapot and handle. This is a good time to put in some background color. I want the violet mid-tones to be a little darker than the background.

7. The next step is to paint the cast shadow and the reflection of the foreground on the bottom of the teapot. I also block in some foreground color so I can check my color relationships.

8. Finally, I carry my background and foreground colors out to the edges of my panel. At this point, I can make the final adjustments to my shapes, colors and edges. The last step is to add the highlights and reflections of highlights. I use titanium white with a very small amount of cadmium yellow lemon for this.

Some Notes on Limiting Your Palette

Limiting the colors on your palette to just a version or two of the primary colors is a great way to learn what those colors are capable of. Fewer colors on your palette will also help you create a more unified final result because everything you mix will be composed of the same root pigments. Take a look at the palette of this project. We were able to produce a very wide range of tones to describe an array of reflected silvers and blacks as well as all of the reflected hues in the teapot with a simple primary palette. Sometimes less is more!

STEPHENS
7·31·21

PUTTING IT ALL TOGETHER

Painting single objects made out of just one material is a lot of fun, and I think it's very beneficial to isolate specific ideas in painting so that we can learn, but eventually, we are going to want to paint something that includes more than one idea. You might want to combine several objects or paint a single object made out of several different materials. The idea is to feel comfortable describing whatever we want with paint.

YELLOW HIGH-TOP

I have a fairly decent collection of old shoes. Many of them were given to me by former students, and a few I've purchased at thrift shops or garage sales. This simple high-top sneaker offers the painter a variety of interesting challenges. Unlike a lemon, which is just made out of lemon, this complex object is composed of canvas, rubber and cord. There's even a little bit of metal in the eyelets.

What You'll Need

- Panel
- Paints: cadmium yellow lemon, cadmium red light, cadmium yellow, cobalt blue, titanium white
- Palette
- Palette knife
- Brushes
- Brush cleaner
- Mineral spirits
- Paper towels or cloth rags
- Ruler

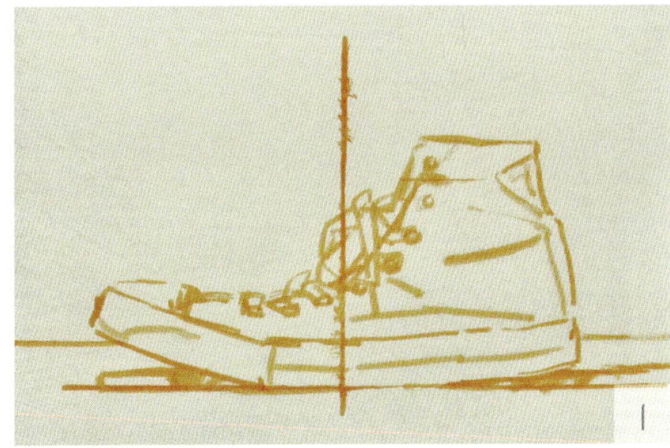

What Do We See?

The most striking thing about this sneaker is its vibrant yellow color. There is a fantastic variety of yellow tones represented. The very darkest yellows in the shaded side are a deep ochre, and those quickly give way to relatively vibrant ambers and yellow-oranges where the yellow shoe is reflecting back into the shadows. The laces are a bright array of small noodle-like shapes, and the rubber sole is made up of a similarly tight value range of light tones. The whole thing sits solidly on a relatively dark cast shadow.

Blocking In Your Subject

1. I start by mixing some cadmium yellow lemon with a small amount of cadmium red light. I then add a little bit of mineral spirits. I find the center of my panel and make a vertical mark to place my shoe on. The vertical axis will also be useful for comparing angles. My first horizontal mark goes at the bottom of the shoe and I extend it beyond the object to help define the cast shadow. The overall shape of the silhouette is a sort of modified wedge. The laces are the most complicated part of the drawing. After establishing the eyelets, I simplify the laces into light and dark parts and draw those shapes. I also want to make some indication of the wrinkles on the shoe.

Mixing Your Colors

2. The first color group that I'm going to mix is for the yellow canvas on the shoe. I start with cadmium yellow and add a small amount of cadmium red light to it. I want to make a medium orange. I add a little cobalt blue to this, which gives me a warm neutral. Right now, it looks a little too brown, so I add more cadmium yellow to bring it closer to yellow ochre. Try to save a little of that darker brown, though. It will prove useful. Moving down, I add more cadmium yellow and then I transition to cadmium yellow lemon. Finally, I add just a touch of titanium white to my lightest mixture. Remember, titanium white desaturates colors, so don't add too much! Moving across from our darkest color, I add more cadmium yellow and a little cadmium red light. I want to match the value of the dark ochre mixture with a yellow-orange that is more vibrant.

3. Next, I'm going to mix the light neutrals of the rubber, laces and inside of the shoe. I start by mixing a medium orange out of cadmium yellow and cadmium red light. I then add titanium white to it until it is a medium value. Next, I add cobalt blue until the mixture is just a little cooler than dead neutral. The goal here is not to turn the mixture blue. I just want to add enough cobalt blue so that it doesn't look orange anymore. I then add more titanium white and just a touch of orange back into this mixture. I want my second version to be lighter in value and warmer. Two or possibly three values should be enough for this job.

4. The final color family to mix will be for the environment—background, foreground and cast shadow. I want another neutral tone, but I want it to have a different character from what I just mixed, so I start with a violet composed of cadmium red light and cobalt blue. Moving down, I add titanium white to get the value in the same ballpark as the bulk of the background and then I add a little bit of our mixed orange to warm it up. This will be my foreground. For the cast shadow, I go back to the top and add a little titanium white to the original violet and then I add my mixed orange as I lighten the value with titanium white. I want to have a good range of values for the cast shadow, from chromatic black to medium gray.

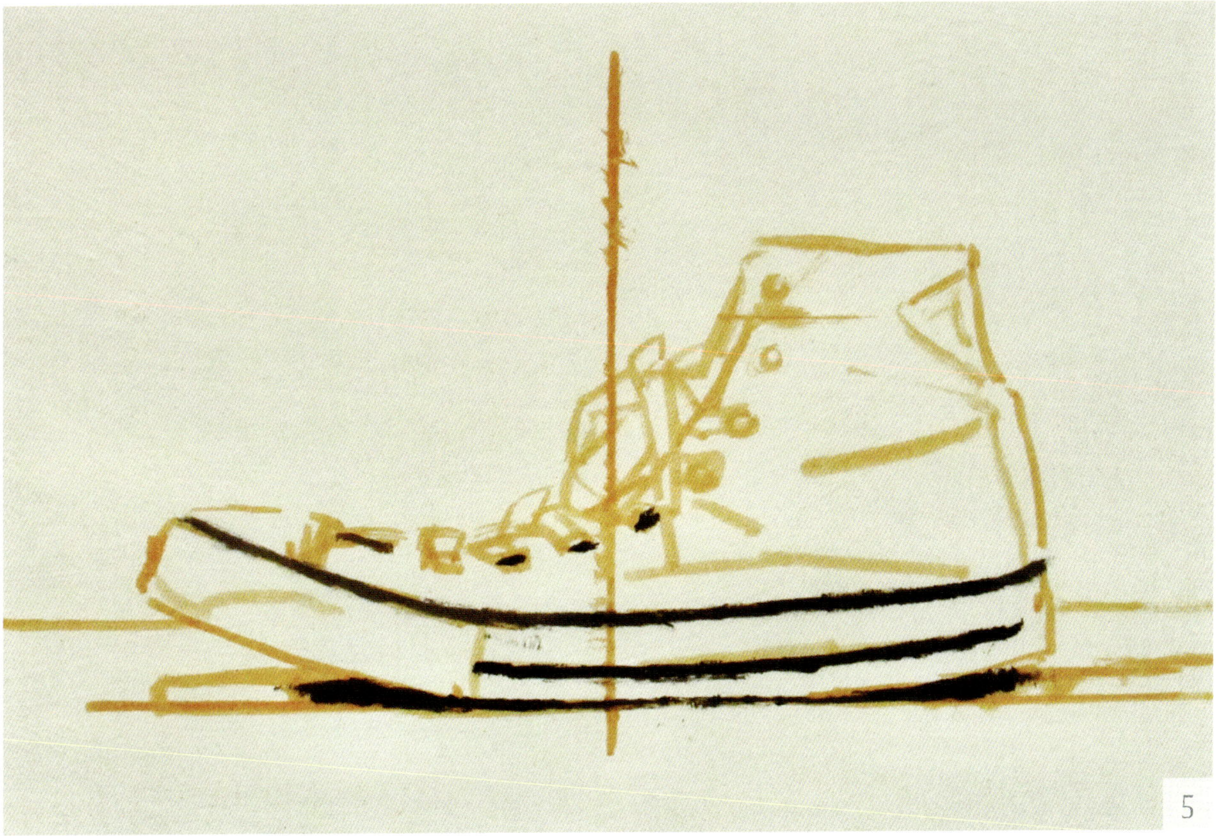

5

Painting

5. I start by establishing the darkest darks. These are parts of the cast shadow and the dark rubber stripes that run along the rand of the shoe. I also establish the small dark accents at some of the lace eyelets.

6

6. The next stage is to paint the shadowed side of the yellow canvas. I first establish the darker and duller areas that don't have any yellow light reflecting into them. I then move on to the slightly lighter and much more vibrant areas of reflected light. During this stage, it's important to take note of which way the planes of the canvas are facing. Generally, downward-facing planes are catching more reflected light and are more vibrant. Vertical or upward-facing planes are less vibrant and a little darker because they're not being struck by the reflected light quite as much.

7. Next, I block in the light yellow of the shoe canvas and tackle that jumble of laces as well as the inside of the shoe. I've simplified the laces into just two values: where they are being struck by light and where they are in shadow. Some of the light shapes will be adjacent to one another and will become one shape. The same will happen with the shaded parts. This is okay. If our drawing is sound, we can count on the viewer's eye to organize these shapes into a coherent whole. Adding some background color behind the laces helps me see the relationships more clearly. It's important that the background color is a little darker than the light value of the laces.

8. Using the same color group that I used for the laces, I rough in the rubber rand next. There are a lot of small, detailed shapes embossed in the rubber of the toe, but I simplify it to just the largest and most obvious shapes. I think two or maybe three values will suffice to describe this element. I also bring the background down around the rubber toe of the shoe. It would be hard to see the light value of the toe if I didn't. I also add the dark edges of the little square of rubber at the heel of the shoe. I have very specific memories of these things coming loose when I was a kid, so I feel it's important to get that detail!

9. Next, I block in the cast shadow and establish the foreground. There's a lot going on in the cast shadow, so I want to be sensitive to the shifting values. Getting the foreground color in will help me see the color relationships more clearly.

10. For the final step, I continue the background to the edges of the panel and add the small shapes that make up the metal eyelets. I can use some of my cast shadow colors for the medium grays that I can see in the eyelets. I use some small, strategic touches of pure white to define the metallic highlights. I also take this opportunity to look at the painting as a whole and to adjust any colors, shapes or edges.

Some Notes on When to Quit

It is in my nature to noodle away at a painting endlessly. I can always find some little area that needs adjustment—an edge that isn't quite right or a color that should be a little darker, lighter, brighter, warmer, cooler or whatever! The problem is that I'm always less satisfied with the paintings when I do this. I have found, through much trial and error, that it is best for me to stop painting sooner rather than later. My general rule is that once a passage starts to read as I intend it to, I stop. Of course, each painter has their own sense of when to walk away, and there are many painters that I admire who bring their work to a very high degree of finish. I don't think there is one right answer to the question of when is it done. With experience, you will develop a sense of when further work will be counterproductive. I have sucked every ounce of spontaneity and joy out of enough paintings in my life. Now, I stop.

STEPHENS
7·31·21

AFTER SCHOOL MILK AND COOKIES

Sometimes a subject isn't quite enough on its own. A single glass of milk is a little spare and a stack of cookies all by itself might seem incomplete. Put these two things together, though, and they elevate each other!

What You'll Need

Panel

Paints: cadmium yellow lemon, cadmium red light, cobalt blue, cadmium yellow, titanium white

Palette

Palette knife

Brushes

Brush cleaner

Mineral spirits

Paper towels or cloth rags

Ruler

What Do We See?

The top of the glass is placed at eye level, and our light is striking our arrangement from the upper left. Our eye level is just a little bit above the top cookie so that the lit surface is an irregular but very flattened ellipse. The milk has an interesting relationship with the background. Notice that the lit side of the milk is a lighter value than the background and the shadowed side of the milk is a darker value than the background. It will be important for us to get that right in our painting.

Blocking In Your Subject

1. I'm using a dirty orange that I made by combining cadmium yellow lemon, cadmium red light and a little bit of cobalt blue mixed with mineral spirits to lay this out. I start with a vertical line in the center of my panel. I roughly place the left edge of my glass on this line. The glass is a slightly rectangular shape that tapers a bit at the bottom. The cookies are just a little bit wider than they are tall. Once I get the big shapes in, I start modifying them and dividing them into smaller components. I make an executive decision to draw my milk glass a little taller than it is in real life. I feel like it fits my chosen format a little better.

Mixing Your Colors

2. I start with the cookie color group by first mixing a medium orange with cadmium red light and cadmium yellow. Moving to the right, I add a little cobalt blue to neutralize and darken the value of this mixture. Moving down, I add more cadmium yellow, and then a touch of cadmium yellow lemon and a small amount of titanium white. These four or five tones should be enough for the cookies.

3. Next, I mix my milk colors. The shadowed side of the milk is relatively cool when compared to the lit areas. I start with a cool violet, which I make by combining cobalt blue and cadmium red light. I then add titanium white to it until it is the same value as the dark side of the milk glass. I take that mixture and add more titanium white and a little bit of my light cookie color to it. This will serve for the warm reflection on the bottom of the glass caused by the cookies. I then mix a small amount of my shadowed milk color with titanium white and a little bit of cadmium yellow to achieve the tone for the lit side of the milk.

4. The last color group I need is the background and foreground group. Since I've already based my two preceding color groups on orange and violet, I think it makes sense to complete the secondary triad and base my final color family on green. I combine cobalt blue with cadmium yellow to get a slightly acid warm green. I then add titanium white to this until I am close to the value of the background. At this point, I can check the milk colors on my palette. Remember, I need this background color to be darker than the light version of my milk and lighter than the dark version. Continuing to the right, I mix more titanium white and a tiny amount of cadmium yellow lemon to create the foreground color. For the cast shadow color, I mix my original green with some titanium white and add some orange from my cookie family to warm it up a little. This is the small blob of cool brown between the lightest cookie color and the light milk color.

5

Painting

5. I start with the darkest parts of the cookies, which include the occlusion shadow at the bottom and the dark shadows in between, as well as the chips. I continue with some of the lighter darks on the shaded side of the cookies.

6

7

8

6. Next, I finish blocking in the lit portions of the cookies. When I do paintings with more than one element, I typically block in the entire element before moving on to the next.

7. I then put in the darkest values on the milk glass. These include the core shadow and warmer reflected light. I also put in the dark accents at the bottom of the glass.

8. The lit side of the milk is next. I also establish the lightest part of the milk, which is the right side of the top surface plane. This is a good time to check the value of the background color, so I surround the glass with it. The transparent glass above the level of the milk is constructed with a couple of different variations of the background color.

9. The next step is to lay in the cast shadows and bring the background and foreground all the way to the edges of the panel. I also adjust some of the value transitions on the milk by adding some intermediate tones between the light and dark tones. The bottom of the glass is simplified to just the foreground color.

10. The final step is to adjust any colors, edges and shapes one last time and to add the highlights on the glass. I use titanium white warmed up with a very small amount of cadmium yellow lemon to do this. It's important to not add so much yellow that the white takes on a yellow cast. I want just enough to make it a little bit warmer. Mixing these subtle tones gets easier with practice.

Some Notes on Scale

I typically paint things close to life-size, but there are times when I make alterations based on my judgment. In the preceding painting, I chose to make the glass a little taller just because I thought it would be more balanced and attractive on the panel size I was working with. It took me an embarrassingly long time to learn that I didn't have to absolutely stick to whatever reference was before me. In my sketchbook, I often repaint a subject at half or one-third scale just to experiment with abbreviating the shapes and colors. This is a good way to see if everything is working as intended. I have also painted small items many times their actual size. It's an interesting exercise to see if you can maintain the energy of a small study when you increase the scale.

CHEESEBURGER WITH ALL THE TRIMMINGS

Cheeseburgers are like snowflakes. No two are exactly the same, and all of them are beautiful. A cheeseburger is a fantastic opportunity to practice depicting a great variety of materials with varying local colors in a compact package. If you paint it fast enough, you may still be able to enjoy eating it when you're finished!

What You'll Need

- Panel
- Paints: cadmium yellow lemon, cadmium red light, cobalt blue, titanium white, alizarin crimson
- Palette
- Palette knife
- Brushes
- Brush cleaner
- Mineral spirits
- Paper towels or cloth rags
- Ruler

What Do We See?

Our light source is from the upper left. The lightest parts of the bun are very close to being the same value as the background. The colors are differentiated by contrasting hues rather than differing values. The meat is very dark, with some very low-key variations evident in the photograph. The lit areas of the patty show a bit more contrast in my live model. The tomato shows a wide variety of reds ranging from near chromatic black to a very pale near white in the highlight. The lettuce is particularly interesting. The greens on the left side are brightly lit. The value is very light and warm, while the lettuce in the shadow is a much darker, desaturated green that is almost a cool gray. The cheese is a muted yellow ochre, and the onion is a warm gray that is very close in tone to parts of the cast shadow.

Blocking In Your Subject

1. I start by mixing a warm neutral tone using cadmium yellow lemon, cadmium red light and a little bit of cobalt blue combined with a little bit of mineral spirits to accomplish my layout. I think this color will work well if some of it happens to be left showing in the final painting. After finding the center of my panel, I make a few marks to place the silhouette of the cheeseburger. It's a little wider than it is tall, so I decide to orient my panel horizontally. Once I have the main shape placed, I rough in the trimmings. I want to keep these shapes as simple as possible. The main thing is to make sure their relative sizes are accurate. I also make a few marks to indicate where the light and dark parts of each ingredient lie.

Mixing Your Colors

2. The first color group I mix is for the bun. I start by mixing a medium orange with my cadmium red light and cadmium yellow lemon. Moving to the right, I add some cobalt blue to produce a warm, dark neutral tone, a dark brown. Moving down on my first thread, I add a little more cadmium yellow lemon to this mixture, which produces a slightly neutralized yellow-orange. Continuing down, I add titanium white and a little more cadmium yellow lemon until I get to a very light warm neutral tone at the bottom. This will be used for the almost white part along the bottom of the top bun. Now I need a mixture for this same local color where it goes into the shadows. To do this, I take some of the dark, cool brown and add titanium white until I approximate the value on the model.

3. For the tomato, I start with alizarin crimson and add just a touch of cadmium red light. I can add a little cobalt blue on the fly later if I need a darker version of this. To get the lighter value, I add more cadmium red light, titanium white and a sliver of cadmium yellow lemon.

4. Next is the lettuce group. I mix a blue-green by combining cadmium yellow lemon and cobalt blue. I then add titanium white until I hit the value of the lettuce in the shadow. Next, I add a very small amount of alizarin crimson. I want to gray this color out a little, but I also want to keep it relatively cool. To get the lighter values, I mix a yellow-green by combining a little cobalt blue with cadmium yellow lemon. As I add more titanium white, I keep this mixture warm by adding more cadmium yellow lemon.

5. For the patty, I mix a very dark violet with cobalt blue and cadmium red light. I use the cadmium red light instead of the alizarin crimson because it has some yellow in it and will make a more neutral violet. The resulting chromatic black will be useful for the occlusion shadow below the bottom bun as well. To get my lighter patty tone, I add a little bit of titanium white and a touch more of cadmium red light.

6. For the cheese family, I start by mixing orange with cadmium red light and cadmium yellow lemon. I then dull it down with some cobalt blue. At this point, I go back in with a little more cadmium yellow lemon and some titanium white to make a lighter version. This color is very similar to some of the tones found in the bun family.

7. My final color group will be the background. I start by mixing some dull violet using cadmium red light and cobalt blue. I then add titanium white to match the value of the backdrop. For the foreground, I add more titanium white to a little bit of cadmium yellow lemon. For the cast shadow, I start with the mixed violet and add titanium white until I come close to the correct value. I then add a little bit of the mid-range bun color to warm it up as I add a little more titanium white. The light reflecting back into the cast shadow is primarily coming from the bun, so this should work out.

8

10

9

11

Painting

8. I start by defining the darkest bits with my chromatic black. These are the shadows in the patty, the bottom of the top bun and the occlusion shadow on the bottom.

9. Now it's really just a matter of blocking in each component. I start with the bottom bun. I paint the dark values first and immediately continue to the light values. I want to make sure the colors work as intended when they are in context. I also establish the dark red shadow at the bottom of the tomato.

10. I continue and give the top bun the same treatment. There are some interesting creases in this element, and I feel like including them would add some interest. I use the front edge of a flat brush to cut these in, but some careful knife work would do just as well. Continuing with the dark reds and moving to the light reds, I also block in my tomato colors.

11. Now I tackle the lettuce: dark and cool for the shadows and warm and light where the light strikes it.

12. I simplify the cheese to just two values, and I try to keep the shapes simple but interesting.

13. I didn't mix a color specifically for the onion, but it's a cool gray. To make it, I just mix some cast shadow color with my cool neutral green from my lettuce family. I can add a little white to adjust the value as needed.

14. At this point, the burger and all of its components have been blocked in, so I add the cast shadow. I'm careful to observe where the variations in value and temperature occur in the cast shadow. To check my overall color relationships, I establish some background and foreground color as well.

15. At this point, I continue my foreground and background colors all the way to the edges of my panel. Now, I can make whatever adjustments I need to make to my shapes, colors and edges. Because I was pretty accurate when I mixed my colors, these are pretty minimal. The main thing I need to do is add highlights to the top bun and tomato and a secondary highlight to the corner of the cheese. These highlights are rarely pure white. I usually mix in a little bit of cadmium yellow lemon to warm them up slightly. In this case, I use a tiny bit of my lightest bun color and cheese color, respectively.

Some Notes on Choosing Subjects

There is nothing like painting often if you want to improve your skills. If you plan on painting every day, or close to it, you will need a lot of reference material. When I was in art school, I had this idea that I needed to make great paintings that had the potential to be historically significant. This was a recipe for paralysis. When I decided I wanted to improve my painting skills and I committed to doing a small painting every day, I began to look at the objects in my immediate world with an eye toward painting them. Scouting for objects soon became second nature, and I realized that anything that caught my interest was fair game. Initially, I was loath to repeat a subject, but I soon came to realize that didn't matter either. Painting a cheeseburger again does not produce the same painting. Every time we commit to describing a slice of our reality with paint, we can benefit as long as we honestly concentrate and become engaged with the process. In short, our state of mind is more important than the subjects we choose. As my former teacher Scott Bell used to say, "Work hard, pay attention and have fun!"

ACKNOWLEDGMENTS

First and foremost, I would like to thank my wife Becky for all of the incredible support and encouragement she has given me over the course of writing this book, not to mention her great ideas about how to organize the text and what to include. It would have been an impossible task without her! Our children, Clark and Maggie, also deserve a mention here, as they have been as patient as they could every time they've heard me say, "Just a minute, I'm writing!" in response to their requests for my attention over the past several months. I'd also like to thank every student I have ever had. This book is a direct result of addressing their questions and sharing their joy when something worked out right. On the other end of the student-teacher relationship, I'd like to thank my tenth-grade English teacher, Rick Brown, who gave me some handy information that I could not have anticipated using so much. Finally, I'd like to thank my editor, Franny, for her patience and all of her positive encouragement. She has been simply wonderful to work with.

ABOUT THE AUTHOR

Craig Stephens is a painter and teacher who lives in northern California with his amazing wife and their wonderful children. He worked his way through college by painting signs and graduated from U.C. Davis with a degree in Art Studio in 1993. Shortly thereafter, he landed his dream job of teaching art to at-risk students at Chana High School in Auburn, California. Craig has since retired from that job and now teaches online oil painting classes from his home studio. He continues to paint just about every day and doesn't see that changing any time soon. His small paintings are available through his website. Craig is also represented by Sparrow Gallery in Sacramento, California, where some of his larger paintings can be found. For more information about classes or available paintings, please visit craigstephensart.com.

INDEX

V

W

Y